⊷ IKE GODSEY ⊷
OF
Walton's
Mountain

Joe Conely

Published in the USA by:
BearManor Media
P O Box 71426
Albany, Georgia 31708
www.bearmanormedia.com

ISBN 978-1-59393-508-5

Printed in the United States of America.
Book design by Brian Pearce.

I dedicate this book to two outstanding women: my mother, Mary Margaret McMahon who always encouraged me to aim high, and my wife, Louise Ann Teecher Conley who has been my constant supporter and loving critic for over forty years.

CHAPTER ONE

For The Want Of A Rug

It was the first day of filming on Stage 26 at Burbank Studios in Burbank, California: June 28, 1972. I had one scene in the opening episode. It was in the Ike Godsey General Merchandise Store. I was selling penny candy to the Walton kids as they made their way home from school.

But my story as to how I *became* Ike Godsey started months earlier. In October of 1971, my daughter, Erin, was born to Louise and me. It was in the second year of owning my own real estate office and business was good. I had twelve salespeople working for me and the future looked exciting. If I kept my nose to the grindstone, our financial future was secure. I told Louise my idea. My acting career, which had sputtered and stammered for years, was about to be put to sleep. I had been balancing my life between acting and selling real estate for ten years. But now, the real estate future was brilliant and I was in charge of great possibilities. My contract with my agent had expired and the time was right. Louise and I agreed that to continue my acting career was an exercise in futility. I still believed that I had talent and my work experience was quite extensive, but I had been following the bouncing ball of the actor's life for nineteen years and had very little financially to show for my dedication other than some pleasant memories. The die was cast! I would no longer pursue the elusive quest.

One sunny day in early May of 1972 I was sitting in my Van Nuys, California office writing ads which would appear in the local papers in the coming weekend. The phone rang and my secretary informed me by buzzer that the call was for me. My ex-agent was on the line. She was all excited that Pam Polifroni, a casting director, who had used me in TV shows for years, had called and wanted me to go on an interview for a new series which was untitled at that moment. I politely informed her

The Waltons clan, from the first season in 1972.

that my mind was still made up; I had retired as an actor. I would go on no interviews, period. She worked on me, telling me that Pam had called her. They wanted to meet me, that it was a series starting on June 28 and sold for thirteen weeks. She told me that I was a fool not to go on the interview. "What could you lose by spending one hour against the possibilities of a long-running TV program?" She succeeded in wooing me from my business-oriented attitude. The interview was set at 11:30 the following day at CBS TV-Center, a television studio that used to be called Republic Pictures.

The next day at approximately 11:15, I pulled into the studio lot and was given directions where to park from the guard at the gate. I still can remember my thoughts as I walked toward the office. I knew that the role was a country storekeeper. I kind of practiced my country drawl, which I had used many times. "Howdy, Ma'am, what can I do for ye? Anythin' else ye need? How about some yams? I got 'em on special? That'll be two dollars and sixteen cents. Y'all come back now?"

I smiled to myself as I readily prepared myself for whatever. As I entered the casting office, I gazed upon the same faces that I had been meeting at casting offices for years. We all had played the sidekick to the leading man dozens of times. Several guys remarked that they hadn't seen me in quite a while. I laughed and made some comment about being too busy to go on interviews. We all lied to each other about how popular we were. I put my name on the "Sign In" sheet and learned that there was no script. It was just a general interview. That usually meant that there would be a "call back" later on when they had a script. As I awaited my turn, I was getting negative. They were taking my valuable time away from my lucrative business. I chided myself to stay positive. I had agreed to take the interview; so give it my best shot. Apparently, I was the last actor called because no one else arrived after me. As each actor went into the inner office, I noticed that the interview lasted about two minutes long. Finally, it was my turn. Pam Palifroni smiled and beckoned me forward.

"Joe, I'd like you to meet Bob Jacks and Lee Rich. They're the producers."

Lee indicated a chair which faced the two of them. Pam seated herself at her desk saying nothing more. Lee Rich told me that the series was going to be on CBS and was based on a "Movie of the Week" entitled *The Homecoming*, which had played the previous Christmas season on CBS. He asked me if I had seen it. I answered no and added that we had a new baby in our house the previous October and evenings were very baby-oriented over the traditional holiday period. That was a trick I had learned over the years. Give the interviewer something unique to remember about you. It worked. Lee Rich congratulated me and asked if it was a boy or a girl. I answered that it was a girl and her name was Erin. They both smiled perfunctorily.

"Anyway," started Lee, "we're in the casting process now. The star of the show is Richard Thomas, a very talented young man. Do you know him?" I said I didn't. He then asked me if I knew Ralph Waite, who would play the father. He informed me that Waite had played a big role in Five Easy Pieces, a recent feature film. Once again, I didn't know him.

"How about Will Geer? He's going to play the grandfather." I knew that name. Lee Rich then paused and looked at me rather oddly. Actually, he stared at me for many seconds. Finally, he spoke. "Do you wear a rug?" His question shocked me for a few moments. That's one question I had never been asked at an interview. Undaunted, I grabbed a fistful of my hair and gave it several stern tugs.

I said, "No, I don't wear a rug. Did you want a guy who wears a rug?"

He laughed and said no. He then went on to name several actors who wore toupees. Once again there was a pregnant silence in the little office. The quiet seemed to go on forever.

Finally, Pam Palifroni broke the communal trance with a phrase that spelled doom for any applicant.

"Thanks for coming in, Joe." I reached out and shook hands with Jacks and Rich. Pam said something comforting at the door and I was on my way. No matter how long I live, I will never forget that walk across the parking lot and my thoughts. I was chewing myself out for allowing myself to be convinced to go on the interview. It took me about twenty minutes to get to my office at Woodman and Oxnard in Van Nuys where I returned to my honest work as opposed to the funny business of TV and motion pictures.

About two weeks later my ex-agent called me and jolted me with the news that I had landed the role of the storekeeper on the still-untitled TV show. I was shocked! The producers had not called to view some films. They made the decision based upon Pam Palifroni's recommendation and the abbreviated interview which focused on my lack of a rug. That's Hollywood!

Over the next few weeks there were negotiations about the contract, the billing, the compensation, the number of shows I was guaranteed and other things. Finally, that was settled. The one surprise was that my ex-agent got the producer to pay the commissions which would go on for seven years, if the show lasted that long. I had never heard of that before and neither had she. When that was settled, I received a call asking if I would like to see The Homecoming. The producers arranged for a showing.

I went over to the Burbank Studios, which used to be Warner Brothers, and watched the two-hour film. I enjoyed it. Patricia Neal played the mother and Edgar Bergen played the grandfather. I had heard that neither of them wanted the hard work of doing a weekly series. The mother's role had still not been filled. After I finished the screening, I was asked to stop by *The Waltons'* office. The creator of the series, Earl Hamner, wanted to meet me.

He had a shock of dark-red hair, and an engaging smile that captivated. He asked me quite a few questions about myself and my career. I did not mention my retirement. He told me about his family and where they were from. I was surprised to learn that the show was based on his family growing up in rural Virginia. I asked a few questions and learned that they didn't intend to use accents. We'd just use our normal speech which would be enhanced by using local names and places. I didn't ask the question about why they replaced the storekeeper. Actor Woodrow Parfrey had played Ike in *The Homecoming* and seemed to me to have done a good job. I was never to learn why. Someone suggested that I worked cheaper, and maybe that was true.

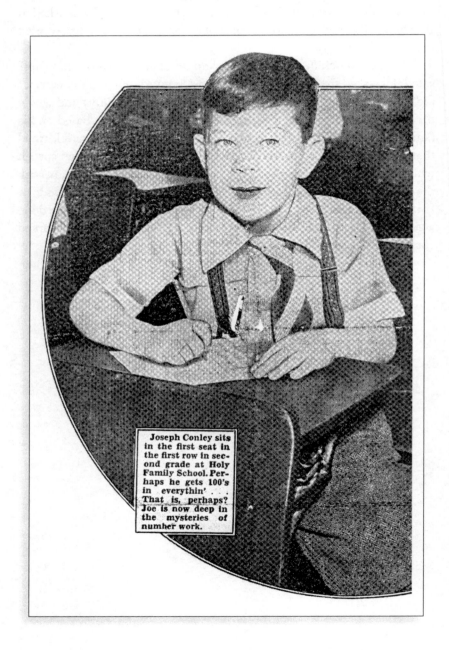

Joseph Conley sits in the first seat in the first row in second grade at Holy Family School. Perhaps he gets 100's in everythin' . . . That is, perhaps? Joe is now deep in the mysteries of number work.

CHAPTER TWO

Beginnings

In 1953, at the age of 25, I arrived in Hollywood ready to start my career. Most actors my age, it seemed to me, already had ten years of experience at my age. But those ten years, for me, were spent growing up, not accumulating showbiz credits.

In 1945, my mother and I left Buffalo, New York, where I had just graduated from high school. My parents, Joseph and Mary Conley, had obtained a legal separation. (Catholics do not get divorced.) My sister, Rosemary, and her husband, Clint, had a one-year-old and my mother came to Los Angeles to baby-sit while my sister worked a full-time job. I had been given my choice to live with either parent. I chose my mother.

When I tell this story, I always add that California was not the reason I stayed with my mother. I would have stayed with my mother if the geography had been the reverse. I loved my mother. She had always encouraged me to accomplish and to aim high. She told me stories of her father, my grandfather. He had been a vaudevillian and had his own traveling medicine show. His colorful name, Snake-Oil Johnny McMahon, explains what he did. As a little kid I was entranced by her stories. Like the "Seven Little Foys," it was the "Six Little McMahons." According to my mother, Johnny and Eddie Foy were friends in New York. Later I was to meet Bryan, Eddie Jr. and Mary Foy, three of the seven.

Arriving in California, knowing no one except my sister and brother-in-law, I was quite lonely. The Standard Oil gas station at Leimert and Santa Barbara had a sign in the window looking for part-time help. I signed on during the first week of September. A boy my same age, by the name of Jerry Toms, worked there also. He was enthused about starting college at Loyola University in November. At his suggestion, I visited the campus, which was in Playa del Rey, and fell in love with this tiny college near the beach. In a matter of weeks, I had my high-school transcript sent to Loyola and I was accepted as a freshman. The first semester was a joy for me. I kept my part-time job and was able to pay my own way. A college education was on the way. I continued to live with my sister and commuted. Along about Christmas my mother and father began to talk about reconciling and, lo and behold, it happened. My mother was

Left: My mother, Mary Margaret McMahon Conley, at about age 15. Right: My maternal grandmother, Agnes Bergeman, with her three daughters (left to right: Louise, Elizabeth, and Mary).

to return to Buffalo and I was to become a boarder at Loyola. I guess we had overstayed our welcome at my sister's apartment.

Moving into the "Big House" on the campus at Loyola was thrilling. The student body was only 500 of which about 50 students were boarders. And the borders were about evenly divided between veterans back from service and kids, like me, just out of high school. My roommate, Bob Buckley, 24 years of age and a veteran, was a senior and president of the student body. He would graduate in June and had been accepted at Georgetown Medical School. I gravitated toward the older guys and loved listening to their stories of their experiences around the world. On March 3, 1946, I turned 18 and registered for the draft. The semester started on March 12. But on March 10, I received my notice for the pre-induction physical. The word was that if the semester started before you got the 1A designation than you would be deferred until the semester finished. I decided to take my chances and started school. I passed the physical with flying colors, and received a letter from the draft board a few days later. The news was good. I was notified that I would not be drafted until July 1. The semester was

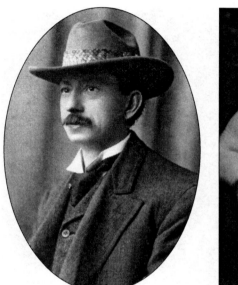 

Left: My maternal grandfather, Snake-Oil Johnny McMahon. Right: Me at about one year of age, in Buffalo.

thrilling as I got more involved with Loyola, my studies and wonderful friends. When July 1 came around I was notified again by the draft board that I would not be called until September 1. I made the decision to enlist in the army. They were going to get me in September anyway, so why not get it over with? I enlisted for two years and, on July 5, away I went.

My basic training was completed at Ft. Lewis, Washington, and then I spent almost a year and a half in Japan serving in the army of occupation. I was discharged in May of 1948 and spent a few months with my parents in Buffalo and then returned to my beloved Loyola U.

The school had changed dramatically during my 26-month respite. The enrollment was now at 2,500 and many new buildings had been built. Joe McAllister, who had been a freshman with me in 1945-46, whom I had also seen at Ft. Lewis, invited me to join him as his roommate in a beach house in Playa del Rey. It was a rambling old house right on the sand. It was owned by Edward Everett Horton, a well-known actor. The rent was $200 a month shared by eight students. Twenty-five dollars a month was a super bargain! The GI Bill paid me seventy-five dollars a month plus books and tuition.

Here I am at at age three, at the beach on Lake Erie with my sister Rosemary and my mother.

Toward the end of the first semester I began to be bored with my business courses and decided to investigate the possibility of changing my major to Liberal Arts. I made an appointment with Father John Connolly, the Dean of Men, to discuss my situation. He explained that if I changed majors that it could possibly take me six years to get a four-year degree. I didn't like that at all and began to think about transferring to another college that had a more liberal elective program. However, I did stay active. I did a play that semester entitled *Heavenly Express*. My role was small one but it was fun. I began writing to colleges inquiring about transferring.

My High School graduation picture, at age 17, from South Park High School, Buffalo.

Notre Dame answered my request, stating that they didn't accept transfers. Several other schools agreed to accept my credits but Arizona State, a school located in Tempe, a suburb of Phoenix, seemed to be perfect. They accepted all my credits as electives, had a $52-a-month room-and-board fee and boasted a second-to-none drama department. I transferred.

CHAPTER THREE

My Movie Debut

The next school year was in the desert. They had a great history department and I loved studying about our country, the world and progress. The drama department didn't quite work out for me. The people seemed too "artsy-craftsy" for me. However, I did get a part in a movie which kind of helped shape my thinking. It was a United Artists release entitled *The Sound of Fury*, starring Frank Lovejoy, Lloyd Bridges, Richard Carlson and Adele Jergens. The studio had hired the football team from ASU to be part of crowd scenes. It was being shot in downtown Phoenix. I went along on a lark and was in the crowd with some of the footballers who were acquaintances. The director of the film, Cyril Endfield, was out in the crowd demonstrating to all the "atmosphere" people what he wanted them to do. He instructed them to jostle a man who was trying to get through the mob.

The director then got up on a ladder, yelled action and talked the scene through as the actor made his way through the crowd. The director was mildly pleased but plunged into the throng once again showing and telling the crowd how to react.

"You don't like this guy. He's part of the authority. You're jeering at him. You're yelling at him. You're letting him know that you don't particularly like him. You're pushing back and forth but not in a truculent manner. You're just a bit unruly. You understand what I mean? Okay? Now let's see you guys act as I come through."

The director began to push his way through the extras, encouraging the gang of people. When he got right next to me, he looked me right in the eye and said, "*You!!* As the actor passes you, I want you to reach out, with both hands, pull his hat down over his ears and yell, 'Flip your lid, short stuff.' Ya got that?" he asked me.

"Yeah, I got that," I answered.

"Lemmee hear ya."

I shouted the line at him.

"Good, good," he said. Then he yelled, "Let's go for a take." Once again he got up on a ladder and asked for quiet, which he got. "Now, when I yell action, you guys do what I told you as the actor tries to get through. Let's go for a take."

Now the cameramen did their thing and then the director yelled for action. The actor came through the agitated bunch and when he got next to me, I pulled his hat down and yelled my line. The actor gave me a dirty look, but continued on through the crowd.

The director yelled, "Cut," and complimented everyone. He then moved the camera around and filmed the same scene a few more times from different angles. Then he moved the camera right in front of me and filmed a close-up of me pulling the hat down and yelling the line.

When the director finished the shot, he complimented me. Then he told the assistant director to call for lunch. The assistant did that and then came over to me wielding a clipboard with a list of names.

"What's your name?" he asked.

I gave him my name and he said I wasn't on the list of "atmosphere" people. I admitted that I wasn't on the list. He told me that I was now.

"And not only that, you get $55 because you now have a speaking part." I was surprised. $55 was like a small fortune to me. I worked again the next night and made another $15. I liked the motion-picture business.

On campus the next day it seemed that everybody knew about my movie debut. School ended a couple of months later and I decided to spend the summer in Colorado. The Stanley Hotel in Estes Park was fortunate enough to avail itself of my employment. It was a funky old place. It was said that the Stanley twins of "Stanley Steamer" fame built the hotel after selling their motorcar company. They moved to Colorado for health reasons. I was hired to be a busboy. It was fun. The employees all lived in dorms and the work was not difficult. And every night was party time. The staff, made up equally of boys and girls, was basically all college students. They were from colleges all over the place. The hotel was building a swimming pool which was to open on July 4. Inasmuch as I had a lifeguard certificate, I applied for the job. But I got cheated out of it. A fellow busboy, who wasn't even certified, got the job. I was disappointed and mad. So I quit. There were loads of jobs available in Estes Park. In fact, the next day, I was hired as an apprentice cook at a local restaurant. I was a bit dubious about my qualifications. I couldn't even boil water without burning it. But the chef/owner said no problem. He convinced me that in a few days I would be doing well. "It's something you'll always be able to fall back on," he said encouragingly.

I was convinced. I moved from the dorm at The Stanley to a kind of shanty located up the hill from the restaurant. I was to start work the next morning at 6:30. The chef dressed me in whites and, I guess, at least, I looked the part. The first thing he did was to walk me around the kitchen and introduce me to all the equipment and supplies. I was lost, but, once again, he encouraged me. Then we moved into the stove and grill area and he began to set up for the breakfast trade. I was his gopher. You know, go for this and go for that. Each time he sent me off I would return empty-handed. I wasn't able to find what he sent me for. I was really frustrated, but he remained positive. "You'll catch on," he said, smilingly.

The restaurant opened for business at 8:00 A.M. The customers began to arrive and now his requests became more insistent and demanding. I could see he was becoming displeased with my total lack of expertise. Many of his requests took three trips until I got it right. His voice was becoming more strident and the volume had increased to the shout level. Suddenly, he changed methodology and, with his right index finger, beckoned me closer. When I got right next to him he turned to me, smiled and spoke slowly, in a new demeanor, enunciating each word with great clarity. "Joe, go to the walk-in freezer and get me a salmon steak. You'll – find – it – on – the – top – shelf, – way – in – the – back. Do — you — understand?"

I answered affirmatively and took off on my quest. About three minutes later, I returned with a frozen piece of fish. He took one look at what I was carrying, drew a deep breath and, once again, beckoned me closer. Then he shouted in my ear, "Salmon is the orange fish. You're fired!"

I changed out of the whites, packed my meager belongings and put them in the trunk of my car before I returned to the restaurant. The breakfast rush was over. The chef gave me eight dollars from the cash register and wished me luck. He didn't say he was sorry. So I didn't either. In fact, as I exited the front door, I couldn't help but notice a big grin on his face. I don't think he was sorry that I was leaving.

Later that day I applied for and was accepted to work on the roads for the Department of Interior. I spent the balance of the summer at that job.

It required little skill, which is what I had. I shoveled gravel and sand into fissures on the Trail Ridge Road up at 11,000-feet elevation. Once again, I lived in a dorm. Life was simple and unsophisticated.

While all this was going on, the world's stage was changing. On June 25 the United Nations authorized the US to lead a contingent of troops from many nations to help the fledgling government of South Korea maintain its independence. Little did I realize that my future would be involved with that "police action."

On one of my last days in Estes Park, I happened to walk by the restaurant where I learned that salmon was the orange fish. The sign was still in the window offering employment as a cook. However, the "No Experience Necessary" tagline had been excised. I wondered if I had influenced that change. I also speculated whether he would feature me in his biography as I have treated him in mine.

CHAPTER FOUR

Quick Change Artist

Arriving back in Tempe, I was more than a little surprised by one piece of mail that caught up with me. I had been recalled into active duty in the army and was due to report in less than three weeks. I didn't enjoy the army the first time. You can imagine my excitement about being recalled. In 1950 I hadn't even heard of the term "networking" but I knew enough to talk to everyone who would listen about my predicament. Someone suggested that I check with the ROTC office; maybe they could help me. Surprise! They could. They enrolled me in ROTC and switched a course so that I would still graduate in June of 1951. When that had been accomplished, they wrote to the army and got me discharged from the reserve. I was safe for a year, at least. I was positive that the Korean War would be over by then and I wouldn't be needed by the artillery. Whew!

My senior year was rather uneventful. Sam Cotter and I shared a studio apartment with the quaint address of 3 West 4th. Small? You had to go out in the hall to turn around. I worked at the Arizona Country Club, played lots of golf and enjoyed my history courses. I turned 23 in March, graduated in May and then left for Ft. Sill, Oklahoma, in my 1936 Hudson Terraplane Sedan which had no reverse or first gear. I always had to make sure that I parked so that I could go forward. In starting out, I had to roar the engine and then very carefully ease off on the clutch before I would speed off in second gear. The car's interior boasted torn and rotten upholstery, which hung from the ceiling like branches from a Cypress tree. My prayers were answered; somehow the jalopy made it to Ft. Sill. After six weeks of training, upon graduation from ROTC, I was commissioned a Second Lieutenant. The Korean skirmish was still going on but everyone hoped it would end soon. I could have refused the commission and I would have been completely free of military obligation. I had been discharged from the army reserve and I was a veteran, which meant I couldn't be drafted. But I felt morally obligated. The ROTC had gotten me free of the reserve and allowed me to graduate.

In early July, I left Oklahoma for Milwaukee, Wisconsin. A friend, Bob Fadness, told me I could get a job easily and we could have a summer filled with golf, Milwaukee beer and lovely young ladies. God was still with me; the Hudson Terraplane made it to Milwaukee where I sold it for junk. I was overpaid when I received $25 for the relic. Bob was correct on all counts. He was working for a manufacturing company called Nordberg Electric as a production supervisor. I applied and they hired me to work along with Bob. It was the cushiest job ever devised. We worked the second shift (3 to 11, five days a week) and did absolutely nothing. We each read a novel a night and played golf every morning at one of the great public courses in Milwaukee. At 11:00 P.M., after we punched out on our time cards, we'd go to a bar in downtown Milwaukee and drink beer until closing. We danced the night away with nurses who worked at a nearby hospital at exactly the same hours. I worked at Nordberg until October 1. But then the cold winds began to sweep off of Lake Michigan and I received notice that I was being called to twenty-one months of active duty. I still felt that the Korean conflict would be over by the time it would be my turn.

I resigned from Nordberg (I don't think they ever knew I worked there) and made my way back to Los Angeles, where I spent a week with my sister and my parents who, by that time, had moved to California. I reported for active duty at Camp Roberts, California, on October 15, 1951.

CHAPTER FIVE
My Korean Odyssey

I was assigned as a Platoon Leader to a Basic Training Company which had no personnel other than a captain, the company commander, and a few sergeants. But in a week or so, we were filled up with draftees. My responsibility was to get our troops to their training site each day. A faculty system did the training. I lived in a BOQ (Bachelor Officer Quarters) and took all my meals either with the troops or in the officer's club. I spent many weekends in San Francisco seeing the town. One weekend I went down to L.A. and my brother-in-law, Clint, helped me buy a car. It was a '51 Chevrolet club-coupe, the first good car I had ever owned. I drove it back to Pasa Robles and it was a pleasure to, once again, have wheels. In early January I got orders to report to Ft. Sill, Oklahoma, where I was to attend officer basic training for artillery. It was a more complete school dealing with the same material covered the previous summer at ROTC camp. Ft. Sill, for officers, was a most pleasant experience. It was a permanent army base where I met fellow officers from all over the country and we visited Oklahoma City or Dallas almost every weekend. However, the ten weeks came to an end and I was scheduled to report to Camp Stoneman, California, for transportation to the Far East Command: Korea. It had finally caught up to me. The war was still going on, although it had slowed down. I felt that I was headed to my death. I wasn't alone, either, with those negative thoughts. Camp Stoneman was just a few miles from San Francisco and it was "party time" around the clock. I had sold my car and could afford a party as long as it would last. After a couple of weeks, I bordered a transport plane and flew to Honolulu and then on to Tokyo. A few weeks later, in early June of 1952, I arrived in Pusan, South Korea. The train trip to Yong-Dong Po lasted forever. Finally, I reached 7th Division Headquarters and was assigned to Battery B of the 57th Field Artillery Battalion. We were in reserve about five miles behind the frontline. We were scheduled to go on line in a couple weeks. B Battery was composed of replacements who, like myself, had just arrived. We trained constantly in preparation for the day when our regiment would, once again, be on the front line.

In about two weeks time we moved out. B Battery, with its 105 howitzers and equipment, located itself in a little valley about three miles behind the MLR (main line of resistance). But my team, composed of Preble Donoho, my recon sergeant, Bob Estes, my radio man, and Willie Brown, my driver, piled into our jeep and departed for Easy Company of the of the 31st Infantry. We were to occupy a position on the highest point of the area controlled by Easy Company. Our specific location was composed of two bunkers, one for sleeping and one for observation purposes. We were in phone and radio communication with our own artillery Battery and also with the company commander of Easy Company. Our equipment was composed of all the materials needed to give artillery support to Easy Company and others designated by FDC (fire direction control) of our Battery Commander. Our sophisticated equipment was composed of a BC Scope which magnified objects several miles away bringing the target to the distance of 100 yards or so. We were able to easily watch the enemy, the Chinese, move about in their trenches as they watched us. We had coordinates of a few locations identified by an elevation or by a nickname. "Hill five niner-eight" (598 meters above sea-level), "Sandy" (a hill that was denuded of vegetation), and a pair of hills known as "Jane Russell" for obvious reasons. It was my job to constantly keep our howitzers zeroed in on a few enemy locations.

Once a day I would call for a test smoke shell to be launched at five-niner eight. When I observed the explosion, I would then call in a correction left or right, long or short, and fire again. Once again I would call in a correction and, with two or three shots, I would have the correct distance and direction due to change of temperature or wind. Obviously, the Chinese knew when I was test-firing and would disappear from my view until the correction was completed. Sometimes the Chinese would then do the exact same procedure as they would zero their flat trajectory guns in on us. The shells would either fly over our heads or hit on the hillside to our front. One never came directly into our aperture but they sure did come close.

That summer of 1952 in faraway Korea was an experience I never wanted and have never forgotten. The weather was warm, the food acceptable and for the most part it was a huge camping trip which I'd never experienced as a civilian. The only problem was that we were being shot at and we were shooting to kill other human beings. Our Division commander, Brigadier General Wayne C. Smith, came to my outpost on several occasions and, looking through my scope, asked me questions about the land to the north and my observations. He dressed in tailor-made fatigues, a shiny brass gun belt around his huge stomach. The gun belt held a pearl-handled pistol that was right out of a Western movie. He was about 5'10" and weighed about 250 pounds; about 60 pounds overweight. Rumors were always in the air that either the Chinese were building up their forces prior to an all-out attack or we were doing the same thing in preparation for our own attack. Nights were especially dangerous. The Chinese were constantly attacking outposts like mine and overrunning and killing all in sight before they would run back over the MLR. One of the officers who was at Ft. Sill with me was overrun and he and his team were all murdered. Our team was on duty all night with a two-hours-on and two-hours-off schedule. In the dark, our ears were fine-tuned to any and all noises. We whispered into our phones, used no lanterns and were in constant contact with all three platoons and with Lt. Knapp, the Easy Company Commander. He was a wonderful man who was recalled from civilian life after having served in the Second World War. We'd sit in the dark and sip our warm beers and he'd tell me about his family back in Texas. It didn't seem fair that he'd be forced to serve again. But I guess he made the same mistake I made by joining the reserve.

After about two months on line, it was our turn to go on reserve. Rumors were still flying about an all-out attack and suddenly it wasn't a rumor anymore. My forward observer team of Donoho, Estes and Brown were transferred to Item Company and the word was that we were being attached to the lead company in a projected attack on hill 598. I thought that this was crazy. Hill 598 sat out in the middle of an east-west valley. The American forces held the southern slope and the Chinese occupied the mountains to the north. Whoever occupied 598 would be shelled night and day. I couldn't understand why we would want to hold that promontory. But, then, I was just a second lieutenant; what did I know?

I was ordered to fly in one of our observation planes to study the terrain from the air. In the piper cub I could see the extensive systems built by the Chinese to provide support for their troops on 598. I made diagrams of these tunnels and was prepared to fire on these locations as needed.

On the evening of October 13, 1952, Item Company moved up near the MLR and waited for dawn. I remember asking a major who was a staff officer about estimated casualties. He told me that they expected 30% casualties. I wondered if I would be among that number.

At 0604 (four minutes past 6:00 A.M.) we crossed the MLR on the attack. My team was with me and we stayed close to the Item Company commander. Almost immediately we were hit with incoming mortars and artillery. At first I thought that it was our own artillery and we were experiencing short rounds. But it soon became obvious that it was enemy fire just as our artillery was laying down covering fire for us. Shells were falling all around us. It was difficult to stay close to my company commander and keep my team within sight. Estes and Donoho stayed near but we lost Brown. I didn't know whether he got hit or had bugged out. I never did find out.

After a short while we were near Sandy and the Jane Russell area with 598 directly ahead. We got the word to dig in. We all carried entrenching tools on our belts and we put them to use in a hurry. Estes was dug in to my left and Donoho to my right. We were safe unless hit by a direct hit. Machine gun and mortar fire went over us. I was in radio contact with FDC and continued to call in fire on all the locations around 598. I was told by FDC that most of Item Company personnel had been wiped out. I was to stay dug in and wait for reinforcing troops to arrive. Time passed slowly but it did pass. But there were no reinforcements. Suddenly, without warning, I saw a solo GI making his way from the rear in my direction jumping from shell hole to shell hole. To my surprise, it was Lt. Col. Isbell. I had met him just a few days earlier when I was back at Division Headquarters taking my flight. He didn't dig in but lay prone next to me. He wanted to know our situation and I told him. He nodded gravely and looked up the slope of 598. Just then Estes told me that FDC wanted to talk to me. I crawled over to Estes and signed on. Once again, I was told to stay dug in; troops were definitely on the way. They were aware of my location. I signed off and crawled back to my foxhole. The Colonel was gone. I asked Donoho where he went. He pointed up the hill. I looked up and saw him about two thirds of the way up the slope, crawling on all fours. The hill had been pounded with high explosives for over a year, the ground was obviously soft as if it had just been plowed. I was transfixed by his bravery. He reached the top and yelled for us to join him. I knew he was talking to me. I was the only officer or non-com in the area. Between the explosions and the rattle of machine guns, I could hear him.

"Come on, men. We can take this hill." He yelled that line over and over. I was being challenged. My specific orders were to dig in and stay until reinforcements arrived. But he was yelling for me and I felt obligated. I stood, waved my .45 and yelled for my men to join me. Donoho and Estes followed and a few other men came out from their hiding places and joined us. There were maybe fifteen of us. I knew I was heading for my death but I was obligated. The flag was waving!

The air was punctured not only by the cacophony of offensive and defensive fire but by the occasional scream of soldiers getting hit or crying for help. As we advanced up the hill, I became aware that our attack consisted of me, Col. Isbell, Donoho, and Estes. The others had either been hit or were hiding in one of the many shell holes. As I reached the apex of the hill there was suddenly a huge explosion, which blew the Colonel's body skyward. He came down right next to me with his body suspended over the uppermost trench. Half his head was blown off. There was no doubt in my mind that he was dead. At that moment the air became filled with hand grenades. I yelled to Estes and Donoho to hit the deck. Most of the grenades fell on down the hill past us but a few of them did their job. I felt a sting in my right hand as I fell. Blood began to spurt from the wound. I looked around at my men and saw that both of them were on the ground. Donoho was grasping his left shoulder where a dark red stain was spreading over his arm and chest. On the other side of me Estes was writhing on the ground. He was hit in the lower stomach area. The three of us were completely ineffective at that point. I looked at Donoho and shouted for him to help me take care of Estes. It was obvious to me that Estes was hit badly. He weighed a ton as Preble and I supported him. I was on his right; Preble was on his left. I said something to the effect that we had better get out of there while we still could. The two of us sputtered and staggered as we gingerly moved down the hill. Shells were exploding all around us as we stumbled our way down. I knew that the three of us were going to be blown to smithereens at any second. But, somehow, God was with us. Near the bottom of the hill, near where we had been dug in for hours, we ran into some GI's. They pointed us further down the hill suggesting that help of some sort was there. The slope

LETTERMAN ARMY HOSPITAL

FOG HORN

Volume XII   PRESIDIO OF SAN FRANCISCO, SATURDAY, APRIL 25, 1953   Number 34

SILVER STAR AWARDED TO LT.

First Lieutenant Joseph H. Conley, recipient of the Silver Star, is congratulated by Brigadier General James O. Gillespie, Commanding General, LAH, who presented the award.

Veteran of D-Day Landing
Heads Dental Operative Sec.

Lieutenant Colonel Lee E. Montgomery, DC, newly assigned to Letterman's Dental Service as Chief, Operative Section, wears the decorations of a Purple Heart with Cluster and an Arrowhead for the D-Day landing on Normandy Beach.

A native of Nampa, Idaho, and a graduate of the Dental Department of Loyola University, Chicago, Colonel Montgomery engaged in private practice in Butte, Montana, for four years before he entered active duty with the Dental Corps on July 1, 1942.

He was assigned to the 49th Engineer Combat Battalion and advanced with that unit onto Normandy Beach and through the Northern France and Ardennes Campaigns.

Since the war, he has served one tour in Panama where, in addition to serving as Chief Dental Officer for the Atlantic Sector, he pursued his hobby of archeology, achieving some interesting discoveries.

Colonel Montgomery's current assignment is his first Letterman tour, but his third within the Presidio area. Sandwiched around his Panama tour were assignments at Fort Mason and Sixth Army Headquarters Dental Clinic. Just prior to coming to Letterman he was stationed at Fort Lewis, Washington.

Accompanying the Colonel to San Francisco were Mrs. Montgomery and their two children, David 12, and Rosemary, 6. Colonel Montgomery's father, Dr. L. E. Montgomery, current as-

(Continued on Page 2)

9 Purple Hearts Presented by CG

For gallantry in action, the Silver Star was awarded this week to First Lieutenant Joseph H. Conley, Jr., Artillery, U. S. Army, a patient on Ward D-2. The ceremony was held in the Staff Conference room with Brigadier General James O. Gillespie, Commanding General, making the presentation. The orders and citation were read by Lieutenant Colonel James F. Clark, Chief, Personnel Division.

The action in which Lieutenant Conley, a member of Company B, 57th Field Artillery Battalion, distinguished himself took place on October 14, 1952 near Kumhwa, Korea. Friendly forces, undertaking an offensive action against a strategic enemy-held hill, had twice been forced to withdraw due to the withering barrage of enemy artillery, mortar and small-arms fire.

When they again prepared to assault the position, Lieutenant Conley, an Artillery Forward Observer, seeing that all company officers had became casualties, assumed command and, with complete disregard for his personal safety, remained completely exposed as he moved among the men giving words of encouragement and comforting casualties.

When he and his men were finally forced to withdraw from the intense enemy fire, Lieutenant Conley refused to accept medical attention for his own wounds until he had seen that all other wounded men had received attention and been evacuated.

The citation stated that this courageous leadership and devotion to duty inspired all who witnessed his actions and undoubtedly saved many lives.

(Continued on Page 2)

ARC Worker Meeting POWs Served at LAH

With the eyes of the world focused on "Freedom Village" in Korea this week, Letterman personnel have been especially interested in a former Lettermanite who is standing by as a Red Cross worker to assist with the welfare of the returned prisoners of war.

Miss Nancy Jones, who formerly served with the Red Cross at Letterman and who is the sister of Mrs. Helen Houston, Chief Librarian at LAH, has been on duty with the 44th MASH unit near the battle lines since January, and is one of the Red Cross workers currently assigned to Freedom Village.

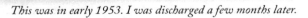

JONES

Mrs. Houston has received no direct communication from her sister since the exchange of prisoners began, but a letter dated April 14 said that she was busy filling "ditty bags" with cigarettes, toothpaste, shaving cream, etc., for distribution to the returnees.

Other recent letters have described Miss Jones' previous activities with the MASH unit. Patients are flown by helicopter from the battlefield to the Mobile Hospital and usually remain only a short time before being evacuated to a hospital further from the battle zone.

The only Red Cross representative assigned to the unit, Miss Jones has sought to perform whatever service is immediately needed, whether it is playing a favorite record, writing a letter home, supply-

(Continued on Page 7)

This was in early 1953. I was discharged a few months later.

leveled off and there, in what was left of some trees, was a half-track with Red Cross markings. A couple of corpsman came to us and took Estes into the vehicle. It immediately left for the rear. Donoho and I continued through a valley as fresh troops passed us going the other way.

In a few minutes, we reached a MASH unit where our wounds were dressed. We were then trucked further back to a hospital and, later that day, I was flown to Japan: the 343rd General Hospital in Kumigaya, Japan. There, I was operated on. A piece of shrapnel was surgically removed from my right hand. I received a little information about what I had been through. The hill I knew as 598 was now being called "Triangle Hill" and most of the 7th Division had been killed or wounded. The battle raged for a couple of weeks until, I was told, another Division took the hill. A few weeks later I learned that our troops were pulled off the hill. It was declared indefensible. I could have told them that weeks earlier.

I met Lt. Gene Barno in the hospital. It was his second wound while he was with the 7th Division. After a few days he was returned to duty. They made him the general's aide. He wrote me a letter telling me that Col. Isbell had been nominated for the Medal of Honor and I had been nominated for the DSC (Distinguished Service Cross). In that same letter he told me that the two nominations had been knocked down to a DSC for Col. Isbell and the Silver Star for me.

I have mixed feelings about the award. I feel honored, of course. But I also wonder about the validity. Yes, I was wounded and received the Purple Heart. But did I deserve the Silver Star? I don't believe I displayed valor. I did my duty for the situation I was in but I don't feel like a hero. I suppose heroism would have required that I move into that trench and continue to do what the Colonel was doing. There is no doubt in my mind that I would have died as Isbell had. I chose to help my men evacuate and thus saved both my life and theirs. If I hadn't followed that path I wouldn't be writing this story today. I understand that both Donoho and Estes returned to active duty in Korea after a very short hospital stay. I was extremely fortunate. I had received the so-called "million-dollar wound": bad enough to get me out of Korea and not serious enough to incapacitate me. I thank God for my life.

I stayed in Japan through January and then it was decided that I should return to the States. I was told there was a surgeon at Letterman General Hospital in San Francisco who had "invented the hand." I arrived back in the "Good Old USA" in January. My parents were happy to have me home and I joined them in their joy. The surgeon operated on my hand but failed to improve the paralysis in three fingers. It wasn't a serious injury. I could still do almost everything. I was returned to active duty in April of 1953 at Ft. Lewis, Washington, but I only had a month to serve before my time was up. I was discharged in late May. I returned to Los Angeles.

CHAPTER SIX

Hollywood, Here I Am

You might ask a question of me at this point. And the question would certainly have credence: "What gives you the idea that you have any special talent that Hollywood couldn't live without?" As a matter of fact, I asked that same question of myself. My show-business experience was limited to three performances on *The Big Brother Bob Show* hosted by Buffalo Bob Smith on WGR in Buffalo. I sang once and answered questions twice. I contributed to the Senior Show at South Park High School. I played a small part in a student production, *Heavenly Express*, at Loyola. I had a one-line part in a previously mentioned movie. And I sang as part of a USO show in a hospital in Japan. Anyone with any common sense would tell me to get a job. But my dream was there and I tried to be practical about it. I decided to give myself three years to get to the point where I was supporting myself in showbiz. Failing that I would go to law school. I could be a lawyer at the age of thirty-one. That was my thinking and I set out to follow my star.

Father Lorenzo Malone was an old friend from Loyola. I called him and he gave me a couple of names. One man was an assistant director working on *Dragnet*, the Jack Webb production. When I called, he invited me to the studio where he described what he could do for me. He said he could give me a job working as an extra. I talked to some people who warned me against that path. Their philosophy was: "Once an extra, always an extra." I listened to the advice and turned down that opportunity. I have often looked back on that day and wondered if the advice I followed was correct. I since have watched many people move from extra to actor.

My parents, who had relocated to Los Angeles, were living in a small trailer in Hawthorne, California. There was no room for me. My sister and brother-in-law had had a third child, Deana, and I was the godfather. They had a small home in L.A. near Inglewood. I stayed with them but it was only temporary. After buying a car I was left with very little cash and I needed a job. I applied to be a detail salesman with Philip Morris Tobacco Co. and I was hired. Fortunately, my territory was Hollywood, Beverly Hills and Santa Monica with a little bit of Burbank and Universal City. With my first week's salary in my pocket, I began looking for a place to stay. I searched through the *Hollywood Citizen News* and found an ad that seemed too good to be true. It read, "Share a new house in the Hollywood Hills, separate bedroom and bath $50 a month." I called the number listed and a guy answered. He filled in the balance of information and then I asked the $64 question: "How do I know you're not gay?" His answer duplicated mine. "How do I know you're not gay?" He gave me his address and we agreed to meet at the house. It was a dream come true: a brand-new house high up in the Hollywood Hills. The private bedroom and bath were furnished very nicely. He was a detective with a large insurance company and investigated claims all over the west coast. He was a big guy, about 35 years of age, and looked rough as nails. I made up my mind very fast and the two of us laughed about suspecting the other. I had two shelves in the refrigerator and we were to wash and put away our own dishes. He told me that he was out of town a lot and the first two weeks I hardly saw him on weekdays. I had the house to myself during the week.

The third week Bob Fadness, my old Milwaukee buddy, was in town. He wanted to get together, but the night he was available I had a date. I called my date and she was successful in getting a blind date for Bob. On Friday I picked him up at his hotel and brought him with me while I showered and changed. When we entered the house, my housemate, Andy, was not alone. He had a uniformed marine corporal with him, whom he introduced as Larry. Larry practically floated as he sashayed across the room and extended his hand in the most feminine gesture I had ever witnessed. I excused myself and left Bob with Andy and Larry as I showered, changed, and thought about the odd situation.

A few minutes later, when I was about to leave my room, there was a knock on my door. I opened it. Andy whispered as he briefly explained Larry. Larry was from his hometown in Indiana and Andy's mother had told him to look Andy up if he ever got to L.A. "It's not what you think it is. I'm stuck with him for a little while. That's all there is to it."

I accepted the explanation and Bob and I left for our double date. A few hours later, after we had dropped off our dates, I left Bob at his hotel and went home. The house was quiet and all the lights were out as I entered the house. I went to bed and slept like a log till mid-morning. I made myself some coffee and was glancing through the morning paper when the phone rang. I picked it up on the third ring. A man's voice asked if Andy was home. I told the caller that I'd look in the carport. "If his car is there, he's home but still sleeping."

I looked out the living room window where I could see into the carport and Andy's car was there. I was telling the caller that when Andy's voice came from the master bedroom. He asked if the call was for him. I said yes and he asked me to bring the phone to him. It was rather an odd request but I didn't think too much of it as I carried the phone, which was on about a fifty-foot cord, down the short hall to Andy's room. The door was open and as I turned the corner there were Andy and Larry in bed together. The scene shocked me. When I regained my composure, I threw the phone at them. A few minutes later, I was in my car and gone. I found a pay phone at the Hollywood-Roosevelt Hotel and in a few minutes I found a room for rent which would take care of my need temporarily. I checked the place out and it was acceptable. Only then did I return to Andy's house. He was there but Larry was gone. At least he didn't show himself. I packed my personal items up which didn't take long. I told Andy that I wanted two weeks rent back. He gave it to me but tried to change my mind. I told him the situation was unacceptable. I was leaving. He admitted he was gay but that he'd never bother me. He said, "I much prefer to live with a straight guy. Our relationship would remain strictly business."

I told him no way. I would not, could not, live with a homosexual. I felt that I was going to succeed in showbiz one day and I didn't want my reputation sullied with the charge, someday in the future, that I had lived with a gay guy.

The next week I was able to rent a very small apartment in Hollywood, across the street from Paramount. My rent was $50 a month and my salary was $55 a week. My job consisted of calling on the retail trade: liquor stores, markets and chain stores. I was to attempt to get displays and prominent signs near the cash register. I worked alone which gave me the opportunity to go on interviews and auditions during the day. I would make up the time spent on showbiz after hours and, on a few occasions, Saturdays. My boss, Marty Maitino, knew of my extracurricular activities and looked the other way. He was a good guy and I did not

take advantage. I had a hand-to-mouth existence but it was working out.
I read the trade papers *Variety* and *The Hollywood Reporter* and followed
up every lead.

My brother-in-law, Clint Kaufer, introduced me to Anne Steele, who
played piano nightly at a piano bar called 'Tis Ours. I began to hang out
there a few evenings a week and sang songs with Anne's accompaniment.
I'm sure I wasn't singing too well in those days. I had no formal training
but I had a zest which people seemed to enjoy. The audience was composed of people who were drinking and, I suppose, after a few drinks, I
didn't sound half bad. I met a few more pianists who worked the piano
bar circuit, one of whom was Don Swander. Don had co-written a tune
entitled "Deep in the Heart of Texas." We took a liking to each other and
soon I was a frequent visitor to his home in Manhattan Beach. Together,
we would record his new tunes. He really encouraged me and would work
with me on holding vowel sounds. It was his opinion that my recorded
voice sounded Negro. He sent me down to Central Avenue in L.A. to
find what he called "race music," especially a vocal artist by the name of
Wynonie Harris. I found one record with the tune "Good Mornin', Judge."
I learned the tune and we would perform it at night at his piano bar.
People would look at me in wonderment when I'd sing "Good Mornin',
Judge." Just a few years later a singer named Elvis Presley did exactly what
Don had prophesized. Elvis took "race music" and ran with it.

Early in 1954, someone sent me to Jack Stern, a voice coach. His fees
were very reasonable and he turned me into a singer by leading me to
standards and taught me phrasing to complement my voice and my per-
sonality. They were almost all "up" tunes such as "All of Me," "Get Happy,"
"The Glory of Love," "Honey Bun," and "Up a Lazy River." Then, in just
a few minutes, he would pen a lead sheet so that any pianist who could
read music would be able to accompany me in my key. I soon had dozens
of songs I could perform anyplace, anytime.

That fall, as I continued to push Philip Morris products, I searched
the trade papers for auditions and sang in piano bars. Somehow, I kept
my body together. I reached the conclusion that I couldn't live on $55
a week. I approached Marty Maitino and asked for a $10-a-week raise.
He informed me that I would be entitled to a $5 raise in six months. I
informed him that I needed $10 or I would have to search for another job.
To my surprise, he got the raise for me. I guess I was doing a good job for
Philip Morris, although my heart wasn't really in it. By the time January

1954 came around, I became thrilled that the Veteran's Administration approved me for a 10% disability. I would get $13 a month. I could eat!

In February, Marty Maitino informed me that the entire sales staff would be going on the road for a two-week period. My itinerary included towns in Eastern Nevada such as Winnemucca, Ely, West Wendover and other wide spots on the road. I told Marty that I'd be unable to make that trip because I had several auditions lined up. He told me that I had no option. All representatives had to cover the entire Southwest during the same period; no exceptions.

My first attempt to get another job was successful. I was hired by the American Chicle Company to do the exact same job in virtually the same territory. The bonus was that I got to drive a 1954 Chevrolet Sedan instead of a panel truck. The shortcoming was that the car stunk of sweet grape gum.

My salary was increased (?) from $65 a week to $250 a month. At least I felt better about the product. Chewing gum was much superior to cigarettes. Although I did smoke myself, I wasn't thrilled encouraging others to start.

Although I successfully made all the auditions, I wasn't chosen by any of them. I began to think about New York. Many people told me that New York was the place for me. There were new musicals every year and I was bound to get one. Then that would be my intro to Hollywood. I was told that success in New York guaranteed success in Hollywood.

I called my old friend and mentor, Father Malone. I told him of my plan to go to Vegas, work for a few months there, save my money, sell my car and then hit New York with a modest bankroll. He thought it was a good plan. He had a friend who was the General Manager at the El Rancho Vegas, a Mr. Lynch. I gave notice to my boss at American Chicle Co. and turned in the grape-smelling car.

CHAPTER SEVEN

Las Vegas Interlude

Reaching Vegas, I was hired by the El Rancho Vegas as a third shift (11:00 P.M. to 7:00 A.M.) busboy. I rented a room for $10 a week and was able to save almost my entire salary and tips because I ate all my meals at the hotel. I watched the early show (7:30 P.M.) at every hotel in town. I would simply tell the head waiter where I worked and a seat was mine. I made it my business to meet every TV and radio personality in town and sang on all their shows. My plan was working to perfection.

Then it happened.

Remember the auditions which aborted my Philip Morris job? Well, about two months had gone by and those auditions had long been relegated to "The Forgotten File." But one of them caught up to me. Apparently, the producers of the show, Eddie Truman and Greg Hunter, had been trying to reach me. I had a phone in my little Hollywood apartment but I cancelled it when I left for Nevada. Somehow they learned of my sister's phone number and called, passing on the information that they wanted me in their production. I had no phone in Las Vegas, but my sister knew I was working at the El Rancho Vegas. When I got to work one night, the entire third shift knew that Hollywood producers had called and wanted me in their show. Everybody was very happy for me but I had no memory of the audition. I had to wait until the following day to call because it was the middle of the night in L.A. In Vegas there are no windows, no visible clocks. And life never stops. I called my sister and she gave me the information I needed. Greg Hunter had called. He and his partner, Eddie Truman, wanted me in their revue, *Going* Up. They had started rehearsals and the show was set to open at the Troupers Auditorium in three weeks. The financial end was rather mysterious but Greg was honest and forthcoming about the monetary situation. Each member of the cast was to own one percent of the show. And I would be

responsible for selling ten tickets at five dollars each. This would guaran-
tee a half full house for one week: six performances. If that worked well
then the show would either continue at the Troupers or move to another
Hollywood theatre such as the Las Palmas Theater. Hunter told me that,
unfortunately, I had to make up my mind that day.

I spoke to everyone I had met in Vegas and, to a person, they all
had the same advice: "A bird in the hand is worth two in the bush." If I
returned to L.A., the New York trip was over. The money it would cost
me to return would cause New York to evaporate. I did plenty of soul-
searching that day but in the end I went for the bird in the hand. I said
all my goodbyes and headed out for L.A. that afternoon. I got as far as
Baker when my car broke down. I needed a water pump. The part came
by bus from Barstow and I was forced to spend the night in Baker which
had a population of 73. By the time the car was fixed, I was almost broke
and another day had passed.

CHAPTER EIGHT

Going Up (Or Down)

I got to L.A. the next day, moved in with my sister and went to the Troupers Auditorium to meet with Hunter and Truman. I found them to be really nice guys and talented, too. I was in three skits and two musical numbers. Eddie Truman promised to write something for me so I would have a solo musical number. I got a job pumping gas at a station at the corner of Wilshire and La Brea. I would work in the middle of the night and earned $1 an hour. It wasn't much but it fed me and kept the car running. Rehearsals were long and rather confusing. The cast was huge and talented and personnel changed almost every day. It was, in many ways, "amateur night." Eddie Truman kept his word and wrote "The Everywhere Train" for me. I thought it was a showstopper. It was highly dramatic and told the story of a guy doing everything to crack into showbiz. It was my story, really, and was a lot of fun. The two weeks of rehearsals, working as a gas jockey and living in a hostile environment on my sister's couch finally came to an end. I never did sell my ten tickets. I guess I didn't have ten friends with five dollars to spare!

The show's demise was too bad because Hunter and Truman wrote some very funny stuff. And the cast was full of talent. I got fired from the gas station job. No reason was given but I gathered it was because the show made it impossible to work the hours needed. *Going Up* went down after six performances. Obviously, I wished I had never left Vegas, but that was Monday morning quarterbacking. I made my bed and now I had to live with it.

CHAPTER NINE

Pick Myself Up

There was a restaurant called Smokey Joe's at the corner of Beverly and La Cienega. I asked the manager if there was an opening for a waiter. He said there was if I was willing to work at all three locations: Hollywood, North Hollywood and Santa Monica. I was available. Smoky Joe's was well known for its barbequed beef, ham and pork sandwiches. It did very good business. The sandwiches cost 89 cents and the tip was usually ten cents. The pay was about seven dollars a day and the tips were about the same. I moved into the Wilcox Hotel, which was across the street from the Hollywood Post Office. The room rent was four dollars a day or twenty-five dollars a week. I changed to the weekly rate with the reception of my first week's pay. Every three dollars counted. Like Vegas, the job included all the food you could eat. After a month I got a small furnished apartment on Detroit St. just off Sunset and my life got back to something more than hand to mouth.

Eddie Truman told me that he played piano one night a week at a piano bar called The Horn in Santa Monica. Coincidentally, it was just a block from Smokey Joe's. I made my "debut" wearing my uniform from Smokey Joe's which was a red-checkered shirt, a red bandana and Levi's. The audience loved it as I sang Jack Stern's standards and Eddie Truman's "The Everywhere Train." The owners were Rick and Margaret Ricardi. Soon, I was singing not only on Sunday night with Eddie Truman but on every other night with the pianist. Irv Lubin. I still went to see Anne Steele, Joe Karnes on 8th St. near the Ambassador Hotel and Don Swander. My life began to change in other ways, also. I discovered that I could become a substitute teacher in L.A. It paid $25 a day and I could still work nights at Smokey Joe's. Rick and Margaret Ricardi had a small apartment in the rear of the bar. They offered it to me in return for doing a few dishes and making a few sandwiches. At that point I had three jobs, was eating well and was able to buy a few clothes, a new car and a TV set. By the fall of 1954 I was beginning to feel comfortable in Hollywood.

Being a substitute teacher was kind of fun. I worked on an average of two days a week. I would be called at about 7:30 A.M. and be given the address of the school. I would usually arrive after school had started. I would be introduced to the class by the principal and the rest of the day I would try to follow a lesson plan, if one was left for me. You would be surprised how few lesson plans were in existence for me. The kids were fun for the most part. Having a male teacher was a new experience for them. In many schools there were no male teachers at all. At 3:00 P.M., I was through for the day, so the hours were great. Along about Christmastime I was approached by Jack Mosier, the assistant principal at Beachy Avenue School in Pacoima. He asked if I would be interested in teaching full time. There was an opening in the second semester for a third-grade class. I said yes, I could be interested but then I explained about being an actor and there might be some times that I would have to go on an interview. He asked me how often that would occur. I guessed maybe one or two times a month. He said that would be acceptable but that I should keep that information to myself with anyone at the school. I said I understood. A week or so later I was interviewed by Mrs. Appleton, the principal. We hit it off okay and I was hired to go to work on January 15. I signed a contract for one semester.

Nights I traveled the piano-bar circuit, sometimes singing at two or three places a night. I remember Joe Karnes exposed my route. One night, when I arrived at his bar with my music in hand, he welcomed me with the following line, "It must be Tuesday; Joe Conley has decided to join us." He was right. I was taking an education class at L.A. State and the class left out at 9:00 P.M. I would go from the college to Joe's bar because it was geographically practical.

At about this time I finally got an agent. His name was Bob Longenecker. Father Malone, from Loyola, knew him from somewhere and made a call. Bob was a real nice guy. His wife was a successful actress by the name of Ruth Hussey. He didn't fill me with confidence, though. "Getting that first job is very difficult," he cautioned. He did get me my first interview, however. It was for a show called *The Halls of Ivy*, starring Ronald Colman. At the interview, I told the truth that

I had a one-line role in a movie called *The Sound of Fury*. I read a scene from the show with the casting director and they complimented me, but they were just being polite. Getting that first show was going to be difficult. I wonder where I had heard that line.

As I look back upon those years now, I have to admit that I was having a ball. My circle of friends and acquaintances grew daily. There was nothing I wouldn't do. For instance, I emceed a midnight celebration at the Sartu Theater, where I told a few jokes, sang to the accompaniment of my tape recorder and welcomed in the New Year ('55) by throwing three packs of cigarettes into the audience as proof that I was quitting.

With a bunch of actors and entertainers, we put together a revue which was to play nightly at a Hollywood bar. Opening night the owner had a banner made which stretched the width of his restaurant. It modestly (?) proclaimed the *Joe Conley Revue*. On opening night almost the entire cast of singers and musicians bailed out. I was left with me, my tape recorder and a trumpet player. We didn't make it to the second night and the banner understandingly disappeared.

I won an amateur contest at Ye Little Club on Canon Drive in Beverly Hills. First place was a three-night stand at the club doing two shows a night. I was paid $50. One night at The Horn, Rick Ricardi, the owner, introduced me to actor Edmond O'Brien and his wife, Olga San Juan. They were having a small party at their home later that night and they invited me. At their home, I met Peggy Lee. She and O'Brien were doing a picture together at the time. I must have spent an hour in conversation with Peggy. She told me that she never vocalized and seldom sang other than when recording. I confessed that I sang all the time: in the shower, while driving, any place. She laughed. I really liked her.

Lou Lang, a graduate of Santa Clara, whom I had met in summer camp at Ft. Sill, looked me up. After his discharge he took a job with Mobile Oil in Los Angeles. He had a friend named Brad Trumbull who was a struggling actor. They had a house on Beverly Glen which had room for one more guy. I seized the opportunity. Suddenly, I was living in a house. I had gone from sleeping on my sister's couch, to a friend's basement, to a hotel, to an apartment in the rear of a bar, to a house in a matter of about three or four months. I still received mail at my sister's house. The post office could never have caught up with me.

After about six months of living in the house on Beverly Glen, Lou Lang quit his job with Mobile and announced that he was moving home to San Francisco. That left Brad Trumball and I paying more rent than we wished. We gave notice and within days we found an affordable apartment in Beverly Hills on Clark Street near Wilshire and Robertson.

CHAPTER TEN

My Angel Appears

In April of 1955 my schedule was still the same, following up every lead and networking all that I could. I sang weekly in perhaps fifteen or twenty piano bars all over the place. Eddie Bradford was a fine pianist who worked at Frascatti on the Sunset Strip. One evening I was singing my heart out with Eddie at the 88 and I was invited to join a couple who were just finishing dinner. They offered to buy me a drink but I turned them down. I explained that I seldom drank. My schedule didn't permit alcohol. They were amazed with my schedule of school teaching, waiting tables and singing. The man, Barney Girard, and his girlfriend, Betty Petit, asked me if I was working in motion pictures or television. I said that I wasn't. Barney said that I should be working professionally. I told him that I agreed and we laughed. After some more conversation, Barney suggested to me that I should come visit him at the studio the following day. He said he wanted to get me started. He told me to come to the old Selznick studio in Culver City at about noon and we'd go to lunch. After they left, I asked Eddie Bradford and the restaurant manager, Jean Belon, if they knew who Barney Girard was but they didn't know him professionally.

The next morning I called in sick to the Los Angeles Unified. I didn't feel bad about it. It was the first time in more than two months and I left a lesson plan in my desk. I was at the studio at 11:45. I was surprised and pleased to find a pass at the gate for me. Barney and girlfriend Betty welcomed me and introduced me to dozens of people. They were shooting the story of "Saint Joan of Arc." It was a segment of *You Are There* starring Diana Lynn. The concept of the show was that modern-day reporters narrated and observed the action of the show and then reported the progress of the story as if they were battlefield reporters. Each segment opened with Walter Cronkite asking the question, "What kind of a day was it?

A day like any other, filled with those events which alter and illuminate our time. Except, "You Are There " It was a CBS show and they used all their reporters just as if they were reporting on the six o'clock news. I met one of the reporters, Lou Cioffi. Barney was the director and I learned later on that he directed all 48 shows for the year and wrote 24 of them; a prodigious schedule. Just before lunch the cast and crew were laughing at one of the actor's lines. It was, "Throw some more faggots on the fire." I think they changed the line. Although grammatically the word meant "a bundle of sticks," colloquially the word suggested something much different. At one o'clock the assistant director called for lunch and within minutes we were in a nearby bar. The group included Barney and Betty, the assistant director and me.

Although they did order some food, the group primarily drank their lunch. Once again I deferred on the alcohol.

At 1:55 we were back on the soundstage and Barney asked me if I had an agent. I told him that Bob Longenecker was my agent. Barney made a face. "You need a hard worker. Let's see what we can do for you. He told the assistant director to get Jack Fields on the line. Minutes later he was laughing and gabbing with Jack Fields. Then he brought me up.

"I have an actor on the stage with me who needs a good agent. I told him about you and he'd like to meet you. Let me put him on the line." With that, he handed me the phone. Jack suggested that I come by his office at 5:00 P.M. the next day. I told him I'd be there. Barney then told the assistant director to get Lynn Stallmaster on the line. While we were waiting, Barney told me that Lynn was the best casting director in town. By that time Lynn was on the line.

"Lynn," said Barney, "I just used an actor on my show here and he's terrific. I'd like you to meet him. Here, say hello, Joe."

I got on the line and Lynn asked me my age. I told him 27 and then he asked me if I thought I could play a teenager. I told him that most people said I looked young for my age.

He told me that he'd like to meet me and asked if I could be at his office by 4:00 P.M. I told him I could. By this time Barney was back at work. I waited until there was a break in the action, and then thanked Barney. I told him about the meeting with Lynn Stallmaster. He wished me well and told me to keep him posted as to how things worked out.

Stallmaster's office was at the California Studio across the street from Paramount at the corner of Melrose and Bronson. There was a pass for me and I was given directions. Lynn greeted me, then took me to his office which was exquisitely decorated with Lincoln memorabilia. Lynn explained that his recently deceased father was a historian. We gabbed about that and what a good guy Barney Girard was for a couple minutes and then he brought up the script. The show was *Big Town*. It starred Mark Stevens as a reporter for a metropolitan newspaper. It was in its third season and was relatively successful. Mark Stevens was also the executive producer. Lynn told me about my character; he was basically a wise guy, a teenage hooligan. He gave me the pages which would be used for the reading then left me alone for a few minutes giving me ample time to get the feeling of the character. I guess I was nervous but I lectured myself, "Be the character, don't think about anything else." Lynn reentered his office with another man. He introduced him to me as the producer, Eddie Rissien. He asked me if I was ready to read the scene and I assented. It was only two lines but Lynn explained this was the opening segment of the show and it needed volume and passion. When Lynn and I completed reading, Eddie Rissien said it was a good reading and they'd let me know. Lynn followed me out and made sure that he had the correct spelling of my name and my phone number. Our visit ended with a hopeful dismissal, "We'll let you know." The reason I thought it was hopeful was that I had always heard the standard dismissal was, "Don't call us. We'll call you."

The next day, at five P.M., I was at Jack Field's office, the Sid Gold Agency. Jack was not there yet. "...but he'll be along in a few minutes; he called in," said Hutch, the office secretary. I agreed to her offer of coffee which she procured for me in between phone calls. Within minutes Jack Fields arrived lugging a briefcase that could test the strength of Arnold Schwarzenegger. His smile lit up the room as he studied me.

"I love your face," he said. "You're unique. You look like nobody else. Barney's right."

He waved me into his office and picked up his extension on the way. The next twenty minutes, he fielded calls from actors, writers, producers, and casting people which seemed to never end. Every call would get his "Joke of the Day." Finally, he told Hutch to take messages and once again he concentrated on me. He explained his rapport with Barney Girrard.

"Most people in this town don't like their work. They don't like the people they work with and do what they do for money only. Barney and I love our work. We love the people we work with and make good money because of our love for the creative process…" He interrupted himself, "I spoke with Barney this morning. He told me you were reading for Lynn Stallmaster. How'd you make out?"

I told him that I had no idea. "They seemed to like my reading but maybe they were just being polite."

Jack heard voices outside his office and politely excused himself. He stepped into the hall and, in moments, returned with another man, a short bald guy.

"Joe," said Jack. "I'd like you to meet Sid Gold. He owns the company. I just work here."

Sid stepped forward, flashed a big smile, and shook my hand with certitude. "Nice to meet you, Joe. I heard you're a protégé of Barney Girard. You got a good guy in your corner." Sid then excused himself. He said he had at least twenty calls to make. The three of us smiled at each other as Sid ducked out.

"Hutch, our office manager, will help you fill out a card. I'll talk with Lynn in a little while and let you know what's going on. Jack led me into the outer office and motioned to Hutch, who was on the phone, that he wanted a card filled out. With a wave, Jack was back in his office and a card was put in my hand by Hutch. I filled it out. It was a standard info card with phone and home address plus my sizes of everything from hat to shoes. I could hear Sid and Jack in their offices making very spirited calls.

Later that evening I got a call from Jack Fields. He had two pieces of info for me. One: he and Sid Gold had a meeting after I left the office and they agreed that they would represent me. Two: Lynn Stallmaster had called; the part was mine. I was to call Station 12 at Screen Actors Guild the next day. I knew what that was. I couldn't work in TV if I wasn't a member and I couldn't be a member until I had a job: Catch-22.

CHAPTER ELEVEN

I'm A Pro!

That April night after I finished singing at The Horn, Frascatti and the 8th Street Grill I slept fitfully because my dreams were very scattered, peopled by Barney and Betty, Jack, Hutch and Sid Gold, Lynn Stallmaster and an unsmiling Bob Longenecker. At 3:30, when I got home from teaching in Pacoima, I put in a call to SAG and requested "Station 12." I was informed that I was to physically appear at SAG, make application to join and pay $200 plus dues before I could work on *Big Town*. I made an appointment then steeled my nerves for my call to Bob Longenecker. He greeted me warmly. I told him about Barney Girrard and Lynn Stallmaster. Bob was happy for me until I mentioned Jack Fields. I told him that I was going to sign with the Sid Gold Agency.

Bob took a big breath and then informed me about all the work he had been doing for me. I said that I understood but Barney wanted me to sign with Sid Gold and I didn't feel that I could go against his suggestion.

"Did you tell Barney that I was representing you?" he asked me.

I told him yes.

"What did he say?" I lied and told him that he made no comment. I sheepishly said, "He just called Jack and practically made the appointment for me." Bob chewed me out about loyalty and I had nothing to say; I was guilty. He finally hung up on me and I felt terribly guilty as charged.

The day of shooting was exciting. I arrived at California Studios at 7:30. The wardrobe person dressed me in teenage-type clothes with a leather jacket. In make-up they put wave-set on my hair and slicked it back into a duck-tail. They had transformed me!

Mark Stevens was star, executive producer and director. I had heard he saw himself as another Jack Webb. He was all-business and knew exactly what he wanted. I had no problem with him. The shooting went well and in one hour the opening scene was history. I had another scene which, I was told, would be shot after lunch. In that scene I had no dialogue. I followed directions, and in minutes, I had completed my first show. Mark Stevens thanked me and told me that the office would let me know when the show would air. I left the studio in a pink haze. I was on top of the world. My salary was $70 before taxes. If you consider the money I paid SAG to be able to work, I lost $130.

Over the next couple of months, at Jack Field's suggestion, I joined a workshop group headed by Terry Becker, a student of "Method acting," continued to sing at "select" piano bars and taught school five days a week at Beachy Avenue School. Jack Fields suggested that I spend a day with him and it was an eye-opening experience. It was his day to drop in at all of the producers' offices in Hollywood. On other days he worked Culver City and the San Fernando Valley offices. He seemed to know everybody. He'd poke his head in producers' offices, checked to see if they were busy, and, if they weren't, he'd introduce me, tell his joke of the day and inquire what they were up to. At General Service Studio he followed his routine and a producer/director named Peter Tewksbury told me that a story was being written and I could be perfect for the role. He told me to go see the Paddy Chayefsky movie *Marty*, and to look closely at the Ernest Borgnine portrayal of the lead role. He told me that when it came time for interviews that he'd make sure I had a chance to read. I saw the picture, loved it, and couldn't wait for the possibility.

In the meantime, I landed a role in a Paramount picture, *The Scarlet Hour*. It was being directed by world-renowned director Michael Curtiz. Curtiz was known as a character and my memory of him is perfect for his notoriety. The scene was being shot on location in Hollywood at the corner of Yucca and Vine Streets. My character was a used-car salesman selling a car to one of the co-stars of the film, James Gregory. I still remember the dialogue. The scene opened with the Gregory character and me coming through the door and walking down the steps of one of those little houses that sit on a used-car lot where the salesman hangs out until a customer arrives. I'm talking as the scene begins.

"What kind of a car are you looking for, Mr. Nevins?"

Nevins answers, "Something kind of nondescript like a Plymouth or a Chevy."

I smile and answer his request. "I think I've got just the car for you."

We then exit the scene off to my right.

The assistant director introduced Gregory and me and we ran the words a few times. It was an easy scene and the two of us worked quite well together. After a few minutes, during which we familiarized ourselves with the sales office, the door and the steps, the assistant again approached us. He informed us that the director was up on a crane and was behind the camera. The assistant told us that he would call "action" and we should run the scene for the director.

Jim Gregory and I went to the rear of the cottage, out of sight and waited. In a few seconds we heard the call, "action." As soon as we cleared the door, I started the conversation as we descended the stairs. Jim and I stopped as he delivered his line then we moved to the right as I concluded the scene.

At that point we heard the loud direction "CUT!" from Curtiz who was ten feet from us, behind the camera on the crane. He then continued to rant at the top of his lungs in some undistinguishable language. When he concluded his outburst and the crane returned to its original position, the assistant director told us to return to the number one position.

I turned to Jim Gregory and asked, "What did he say?" Jim shook his head and said that he hadn't the foggiest.

I then asked Jim what he thought we should do. He answered with a shrug and the suggestion that perhaps we should do the scene with a little less pace; slow it down. I nodded in agreement and, in a minute or two, a camera man announced the number of the scene, that it was Take #1 and banged the slate. This was to be a take. The assistant yelled action and Jim and I moved through the door. We played the scene as written but perhaps just a mite slower. As we moved off to the right we heard, "CUT." Then once again a stream of absolutely undecipherable sounds came from Mr. Curtiz.

The assistant instructed us to take it easy for a few minutes while they set up the next scene. Perhaps ten minutes later the assistant led us over to an exit from the car lot and explained that Jim was to drive a grey-green Plymouth off the lot. I was to wave as the car passed me and exited onto Vine St.

We did the scene as explained without incident. The assistant once again approached me and told me that Mr. Curtiz would like to speak to me. He pointed off and said, "Mr. Curtiz is sitting on the curb over there."

I approached Mr. Curtiz, who appeared to be watching ants run back and forth. I cleared my throat to announce my arrival. Mr. Curtiz motioned that I was to join him on the curb. He then made the following statement in barely understandable English. I think the accent was Hungarian.

"You are a vunderfull actor. I will use you in all my pictures."

He then returned to his study of the ants and I concluded that our conversation was completed. That was my experience of working with the world-renowned Hungarian director Michael Curtiz. I never heard from him again. The picture? Someone told me that it was to be a starring vehicle for one of Paramount's new stars, Carol Ohmart. I had never heard of her or about the picture again.

"I moved every time the rent was due," was a joke about the credibility of actors. However, at that time of my life it was pretty close to true. With the teaching money coming in regularly and acting jobs becoming more frequent, it became possible for me to get an apartment. I found one on Formosa St. near Santa Monica and LaBrea. I did a few days' work on a feature titled *Screaming Eagles*, a war story, and then I did a small role on *The Lineup*, a very popular TV show. I kid you not, one of my lines was, "I was framed." The assistant director on that show was Jesse Lasky, Jr., a son of one of the founders of Paramount Pictures. He predicted a big career for me in the future. I was getting more confidence and things were happening. I got word from Jack Fields in August that the reading was coming up for that *Marty*-type role. I was a little nervous for the reading but apparently the producer was happy and I was set for the guest lead in an episode of *The People's Choice* starring Jackie Cooper.

As I remember the storyline, Jackie's character, Sock, had been elected a councilman in a small town. His girlfriend, played by Patty Breslin, character's name was Mandy Peoples. Thus, the title of the show: *People's Choice*. Paul Maxey played the Mayor and what made the show different was that Sock has a dog, a Basset Hound, with large soulful eyes. This dog, a female, had a sarcastic opinion on everything and spoke English. Only the audience heard the comments.

I played Ernie, who was a fix-it man and personal friend of Sock's. Sock's secretary, Myra, has no secretarial skills. Sock plays cupid and arranges a blind date for Ernie and Myra hoping that, if they marry, Sock will accept her resignation. The filming went well and everyone seemed pleased with the show and with my performance. A few weeks later, when the show aired, it did quite well in the ratings. Shortly after that I was informed by Jack Fields that they were writing another episode with Myra and me after we are married and a baby is on the way. That show went well also and a few weeks later Jack Fields notified me that they wanted Tamar Cooper (Myra) and me to be under contract. I signed the contract and everything was wonderful as we went into the Christmas holidays. I was about to become a co-star on a weekly comedy show in my first year in the business. However, it didn't quite work out that way. Tamar Cooper wouldn't sign the contract. It seems that her agent had aspirations for a movie career. Although I had signed the contract, it was null-in-void in the event that Tamar didn't sign. I met her years later on an interview and although she didn't say it, I could read between the lines that she regretted turning down the *People's Choice* contract.

January 1956 started out with a bang. Barney Girrard cast me in a wonderful role playing a living man, Corporal James Larney, who served in the "Fighting 69th" and was involved with that organization when they were trapped behind the lines by the Germans in the winter of 1944. I had some very dramatic scenes and Barney was pleased with my performance. When that episode of *You Are There* played, I received a letter from James Larney himself, thanking me for my portrayal.

The next month, February, I was cast in a pilot film which, had it sold, would have given me a regular role in an adventure series entitled *Treasure Hunt*. However, it didn't sell.

In June of that year, Gerd Oswald, the director of a picture starring Barbara Stanwyck, *Crime of Passion*, cast me in an unlikely role. I played a delivery boy from a Jewish deli. Gerd, who was Jewish, got a kick out of having me play that role. I met him while entertaining at The Horn. Gerd used to kid me about being "a nice Irish boy in a Jewish business."

Singing at The Horn provided me with introductions to many people in show business and they responded by giving me work.

You, the reader, must be wondering, at this juncture, about my activity with the opposite sex. I remember mentioning the double date I arranged when I was living with Andy in the Hollywood Hills. And now, as I look back over the years between '53 and '56, I can't remember a single date. I was so fiercely dedicated and committed to making it in show business that love life had no space. My parents were living in Hawthorne and my sister was in L.A. not far from Inglewood. Many Sunday afternoons and evenings I spent with my family. They cheered me on but wondered if I was wasting all that youthful dedication in a field that would never reward me for that commitment. Every waking hour I was thinking about how I could advance myself in my chosen field. Almost every night I still sang in piano bars, primarily at The Horn, where I had become a crowd favorite. One night, when I had finished my three-song set, a man introduced himself to me, gave me his card and said that he would like to offer me a job. His company was in liquor and spirits. The job he offered was as a salesman calling on restaurants, bars and retail liquor stores. He told me that I would make about $1,000 a month, which was about three times what I made teaching and acting. I accepted his offer quickly, but he had a condition. I would have to give up my showbiz aspirations. I would have to be just as committed, just as devoted, to liquor sales, as I was to show business.

I told him that I couldn't do that. He told me that the offer was an open one.

"You let me know and the job is yours."

It certainly gave me cause to think. Here I was with no love life, no guarantees, and uncharted years ahead. But my life was exciting; something happening all the time.

Sometime, later in 1956, Brad Trumbull and I moved to a much larger apartment in Hollywood along with Chuck Ireland, a friend of Lou Lang's and a very nice guy.

One night, at The Horn a fellow singer told me that Horace Heidt, a nationally known orchestra leader and producer, was holding auditions at the brand-new Beverly Hilton Hotel. I got the particulars and a week later I was on the stage at the Hilton with Horace Heidt seated at a table in the cavernous dining room. I did a three-song set with a little chatter in between. When the audition was over, he invited me to join him at his table. He said I was one of the best bass voices he had ever heard. I knew he was attempting to compliment me, but I corrected him. "I'm a baritone," I informed him.

He then corrected me. "I've been auditioning singers for thirty years and if I say you're a bass, you're a bass."

I remained quiet while he continued. "Do you do 'Minnie the Mermaid' and 'Popeye, the Sailor Man'?" I told him no. He then concluded the conversation by telling me to learn those two songs and then come back and sing them for him. "If I like them, I'll hire you."

I went to Schirmer's music store and they ordered the sheet music for me. Eddie Bradford set the key which allowed me to sing at my best and recorded the accompaniment on my tape recorder. I learned the songs and then arranged for him to play for me at the second audition. I then had over $60 invested. I sang the tunes for Heidt and he applauded from his table, and then beckoned me down to his table once again. He told me that I was hired. I'd start the following Saturday night and I'd be paid $50 a week. He asked me if I had "charts" for the new tunes. I told him no. He then informed me that his arranger would do the charts for about ten dollars. The "charts" are music for each member of the orchestra.

I called everybody I knew in the world. This was to be my opportunity to perform on the big stage at the Hilton with a full orchestra background. Barney Girard and Bette Pettit would be there and several others. At the rehearsal, Horace told me that I'd be doing "Minnie" and "Popeye" only. I was disappointed that my strong numbers were not to be included in my act.

On Saturday night Horace told the audience that he loved my bass voice and that that he discovered "Jumpin' Joe Conley" when he was touring in Arizona. The new tunes went all right but there was not a great audience reaction; just polite applause. Sunday night just before I went on, he told me to drop the new tunes and go back to my regular music. I did not have "charts," though, and I was forced to sing with piano, bass and drums with only the piano man working with a lead sheet.

At the end of my first week I got my paycheck from Horace himself. He paid everyone personally. I noticed that he had deducted $15 for charts on "Popeye" and Minnie." I questioned him about the deduction. I said, "You told me it was going to be $10 for the charts." He answered me curtly, "I said *about* ten dollars."

Before I could say anything more, he told me that I was fired. "Your last show is tonight." I had heard that Horace was cheap but I didn't think he'd be that tight.

About that time I met Mark Newman at The Horn. He was a brother of Alfred and Lionel Newman, legendary musical directors at 20th and MGM. Mark was an agent. He asked me if I would be interested in doing a TV pilot at Columbia. He represented Paul Gilbert, a nightclub comic and star of the new series *Shore Leave*. Of course, I answered in the positive. I gave him my phone number and a few days later he called me and set up an interview with Harry Sauber, the producer. The interview was quick and I was hired. I tried to pay Mark Newman a commission but he refused to accept it. A couple of weeks later we were shooting the pilot film, which was intended to be a navy *You'll Never Get Rich*, the Phil Silvers hit series. It had many very funny sequences and, of course, we all hoped it would be picked up by one of the networks. Peter Marshall was the second banana. He later went on to immortality as the host of *The Hollywood Squares*. During the filming we got quite close and when we meet today it's still a pleasant time. That show was my last performance of the year and I felt quite pleased with my progress.

During 1956 I had done nine TV shows, two motion pictures and one abbreviated singing gig with the strange Mr. Heidt. Of course I was still singing 350 nights a year at The Horn or some of my other favorite piano bars.

CHAPTER TWELVE

I'm Off And Running!

1957 started off well as I continued to do motion pictures and TV. During that year I did TV shows such as *Dragnet, The Danny Thomas Show, Boots and Saddles* and *The Silent Service.* I appeared in several motion pictures including one entitled *Juvenile Jungle,* where I had a co-starring role. I also ventured into new areas of showbiz. I did my first commercial for Gem Razors, which proved to be quite lucrative. I also did background singing for a major film. How I got into that situation is an interesting story.

One day I got a phone call from a woman who stated that she was an assistant to Ray Henderson at Universal Studios. She wanted to know if I was available on October 21 for background singing for the picture *Never Steal Anything Small.* I asked her if she had called my agent. She said no. I told her I'd have to call her back after I checked with my agent. I then called Jack but he was unavailable. I spoke with Hutch, the office manager, who admitted that she knew of no Ray Henderson and wasn't familiar with background singing. I asked her if I should accept the job. Her opinion was that I had nothing to lose.

I then called Universal back and confirmed that I would be at Stage 7 on the appointed day and designated hour.

When I arrived, I saw a few singers that I knew from The Horn. Primarily they were background singers. They all read music and needed little or no rehearsal time. Ray Henderson introduced himself to me and the mystery unraveled. He was a patron at The Horn and was just giving me an opportunity to pick up a few bucks. I told him that I didn't read music. He said that didn't matter. "Just sing along with the rest of the guys," was his offhand advice.

So that's what I did through a couple of numbers. At about 10:00 A.M. a group of about six or seven men entered the soundstage at a far door,

Dragnet *stars Ben Alexander, Jack Webb, and I in 1957.*

perhaps one hundred feet from where I was clustered with the rest of the singers. Ray Henderson introduced the group to the singers. They were actors in the film who would lend their untrained voices to a few of the chorus songs. I recognized a couple of the actors, Royal Dano and Billy M. Greene. I knew them from other pictures or interviews. The star of the picture, Jimmy Cagney, was there also. Suddenly, I knew that I didn't want to be seen by Jimmy Cagney as a background singer. I hid behind other men and kept the music up in front of my face so that I wouldn't be rec-

Another Dragnet *photo: with Jack and Ben and a couple of unknown (to me) actors.*

ognized. Henderson was listening to a playback. He would either accept it as a "take" or request another recording with some specific changes. I was seated during the playback with the sheet music covering my face. Suddenly, I was aware of footsteps coming toward me. The feet stopped right in front of me. I looked up and saw a smiling Jimmy Cagney who said, "I was watching TV last night and saw you on *Dragnet.* You are a very good actor."

He was correct; the show did play the previous night. That anyone of the stature of Jimmy Cagney would make such a comment shocked me. But I was still embarrassed to be caught doing background singing and I began to apologize and attempted to explain my presence.

Cagney knew exactly what I saying but he wasn't buying my thinking. He then began to tell me about his run-in with the Warner Brothers. "But they couldn't beat me because I had the biscuit."

He used that word a couple of times and I finally had to ask him what he meant by the "biscuit."

I got co-star billing in this Republic Picture in 1957. Rebecca Wells is the dark-haired girl, and the guys are Dick Bakalian and Jo Di'reta.

"Money in the bank, that's what the biscuit is. As long as I had money in the bank they couldn't force me to do pictures I didn't want to do."

At that point Ray Henderson was telling the singers what he wanted and Cagney whispered, "Hang in there. You got what they need — talent."

I was always happy that I took that job. Not only was I able to pay my rent that month but I was complimented by one of the all-time showbiz greats.

1957 ended with me doing four pictures, seven TV shows and one commercial. Hollywood was beginning to know who Joe Conley was. At least I hoped so.

1958 started out with me getting a plum of a job. I played a town idiot in a Western starring Arthur Kennedy. Kennedy had won a Tony for his portrayal as "Biff" in Arthur Miller's *Death of a Salesman*. The reason it was a plum role is that I was a sidekick to the lead who played a blind gunfighter. That's right, a blind gunfighter. The script was so unusual that CBS brought in Richard Whorf to direct. Mr. Whorf was well known as a troubleshooter. What surprised me was the answer I got from Arthur

TV show December Bride *with Spring Byington, me, and Verna Felton.*

Kennedy when I asked him why he accepted the role. I was expecting an answer which would regard the complexity of the character, etc. Instead, his answer was, "I got two offers at the same time; this show and *Playhouse 90*. This show was five days' work; *Playhouse 90* was 16 days — same money!"

I don't believe the film ever played. Could you believe a show about a blind gunfighter? Hollywood is strange.

The second show I did in 1958 was *The Life of Riley* starring William Bendix. It was a teenage story and my girlfriend in the show was played by Jill St. John who was an up-and-coming young starlet. Because she was under eighteen years of age, by law she had to have a welfare worker on the set protecting her. What was laughable was that she had already

Barry O'Hara and I about 1959. We never did get our act together.

been married and divorced. Yes, Hollywood *is* strange!

1958 had me doing fifteen TV shows, among them *Studio One* and *Playhouse 90*, prestigious shows shot live. I had to join AFTRA, my second showbiz union. I also did a small part in *Pork Chop Hill*, a Korean War film, directed by Lewis Milestone, a world-renowned writer and director. He had directed *The Front Page, All Quiet on the Western Front*, many other films. My part was so small that it was directed by an assistant director. I never did meet Mr. Milestone.

In that year I began to study with Jeff Corey. His classes were filled with people who eventually became some of the biggest stars in Hollywood. I can remember being in class and doing scenes with Jack Nicholson, Mike Connors, James Coburn and many more. Jeff was a good guy and a talented director. He had been blacklisted by the studios because he was declared un-American by HUAC. I later was to meet and work with another blacklisted actor, Will Geer.

1959 started off with a Jack Webb Production entitled *The D.A.'s Man*. I played a "way out" musician who was also a druggie. Jack Webb wrote my dialogue and appeared on the set and took over direction from the

Les McCann and I in a TV show entitled The D.A.'s Man, *about 1960. I played a doper named "Specs."*

director. In several appearances on *Dragnet* I had had no problem with him but on this show he was quite critical of me. He finally walked off the stage in a huff. I had the distinct feeling that he would have liked to fire me but that would entail hiring another actor and reshooting two days of filming. His business sense took over. I received many positive comments on my performance in that show but not from Mr. Webb. You can't please everybody!

January 29 was a wedding day. Jacqueline Stakes and Joseph Conley tied the proverbial knot at Blessed Sacrament Church in Hollywood. We had been dating for over two years. Two children came of this union;

Kevin born on July 19, 1960 and Julie born June 27, 1961. The marriage was not made in heaven and ended in divorce several years later. I will not use this occasion to document the blame. The marriage just didn't work for either of us.

Let's go back to showbiz. 1959 proved to be a very good year for my career. That year saw me do two more episodes of *Playhouse 90*, many TV shows, a commercial and I was also hired to write a *Dennis the Menace* story. That really thrilled me. I saw myself moving into the creative end of television. Although I had a few sputtering successes as a writer, I was not to be another Ernest Hemingway.

One interesting job I had was on the TV show *Wanted: Dead or Alive*, a Western starring Steve McQueen. The set was a troubled one. There was no laughter, no fun on the set. I had several scenes with Steve. He never introduced himself. He never indulged in any conversation. He was almost always late on the set. James Coburn, an acquaintance from Jeff Corey's class, told me about the unhappy set. He and Steve were buddies, having done *The Magnificent Seven* together. He told me that Steve wanted out of the show and the producers wouldn't let him out. Ergo, the unhappy set.

A happy set was one with David Janssen. The show was called *Richard Diamond, Private Detective*, and, obviously, the producer liked me. He cast me as a bartender who passed on messages to Richard. Obviously, this was before cell phones and pagers. The show played on all three networks over three seasons and I rode along.

Toward the end of 1959, I had an interview with the director of a TV show entitled *Alcoa Presents*. It was an anthology and quite successful. The interview was with Elliot Silverstein. When I entered the little office, Silverstein stood up and said that I should have his seat and I should be interviewing him. Then he actually moved around and took the actor's seat. He really impressed me. Or, rather, he flattered me and I wasn't used to it. I was to play a crooked son of a crooked father in the deep uncomplimentary South. Cliff Robertson was the star and my father was played by John Marley. I was beginning to move in select company.

Later that year I did my second *Danny Thomas Show*. Sheldon Leonard directed it and was as fast moving as anything I ever did. Danny, although he was very foulmouthed, was a genius when it came to finding humor in almost everything. He and Sheldon rewrote and tweaked the script for three days up until show time and beyond. It was the happiest set I ever

Cliff Roberton and I doing a scene on Alcoa-Goodyear Presents *in 1961.*

encountered. No wonder Danny went on to be producer and director of more than a dozen TV series.

All this time, when I was getting "my feet wet" in Hollywood, I was playing golf. I usually played at Griffith Park or Rancho, which was just down the street from 20th Century-Fox. Occasionally, I would play at a brand-new city course located in the San Fernando Valley. It opened in 1954 and I still play there once in awhile. I met a few actors while playing, among them Bill Mims who introduced me to Peter Hansen, a graduate of the prestigious Pasadena Playhouse. Peter had been under contract to Paramount. He knew many people. When he learned that I was writing a screenplay about the Korean War he arranged a golf game with Jerry Hopper, a distant relation of Hedda Hopper, who was under contract to Paramount as a director. Jerry wanted to read what I had written and was very encouraging. I worked hard at my writing and became very close to Jerry as he helped me make writing decisions. Supposedly this would work out for all of us. Peter Hansen would play Lt. Knauf, the infantry company commander, Jerry would direct and I would write.

Suddenly, I got word that I had been set to play a major role in a Paramount Picture entitled *Blueprint for Robbery*. It was three weeks' work and I would earn a big chunk of change. Then I discovered the source of this role. Jerry Hopper was directing. In the film, which was loosely based on the unsolved Brinks robbery, I played one of the robbers. The role was definitely a supporting role and, if successful, could lead to bigger and better roles for me. Although Jerry and I were to become lifelong friends, the plan to make *The Retread* never did come about. He died in the mid-1980s and his family gave me the honor to deliver his eulogy.

One of the many television shows I did in 1960 was *Adventures in Paradise*. The source of this job was once again from singing at The Horn. Tony Muto, a regular patron at The Horn, was the producer of *Adventures in Paradise* starring Gardner McKay. I not only did the show, which had me playing a Hawaiian surfer, but it led to an assignment to write an article for a fan magazine. I was to do a half dozen of these articles which all went to help pay the rent.

In November I got the biggest surprise in years. Jack Fields called and told me that I had been set for a movie at 20th. The title was *All Hands on Deck* and it starred Pat Boone and Buddy Hackett. It seems that a cast member by the name of Hal Riddle cancelled out at the last minute and Sid Gold was there at the right moment. The money was terrific and I would have six weeks' work. Wow! The part was nothing to write home about, however. I had a line here and a line there. But I earned more money on that show than I had made the whole year. I got to know Buddy Hackett pretty well and whenever we ran into each other (and we did often) it was old home week. Norman Taurog directed with very little originality. It was Pat Boone's fifth picture. He was a very friendly guy. I still see him occasionally at celebrity golf tournaments. One day,

Blueprint for Robbery

SUCCESSFUL MULTI-MILLION DOLLAR holdup leads to hoodlums Jay Barney and Joe Conley fighting over spoils in "Blueprint for Robbery," drama of a gang and it's carefully laid and rehearsed plan to rob an armored car service in Boston. Conley draws a gun and demands his share of loot from Barney, who masterminded the highly complex scheme in the Paramount film drama which was produced by Bryan Foy.

I played one of the robbers in Blueprint for Robbery *in 1960. My friend Jerry Hopper directed.*

while we were shooting on the lot, I met Elvis Presley. Jack Grinnage, who was *on All Hands on Deck* with me, had done *King Creole* with Elvis. He introduced us on the set. That day Elvis was breaking boards with his hands. He had been studying karate and was practicing his craft. He was very friendly.

But the good news of the long job and the good money lost all joy when my dad suddenly died on December 31. He had been living in Yucaipa, near Hemet, and really liked it. He was trying to talk my mother into joining him there but she wanted to stay in L.A. to be near the grandchildren. My dad went to a quack doctor with a back ailment which really

A publicity photo from All Hands On Deck, *starring Pat Boone and Buddy Hackett.*

was a ruptured spleen. He was a healthy man who died way before his time. I visited with him just before he passed on and his last words to me were, "You've been a good son!"

In January of 1961 I was back at work on a new series called *Acapulco* starring Jimmy Coburn. John Robinson, the producer, had used me as the bartender on *Richard Diamond, Private Detective*, now had me playing the same role at a joint called "Bobby's Place." Bobby was played by Bobby Troup, the songwriter. A few of his big hits were "Route 66," "Lemon Twist" and "Daddy." He was a great guy with tons of stories and could he drink! He'd put away three martinis at lunch. I stuck with coffee. Another couple of actors on that show were Telly Savalas and Jason Robards, Sr. They were exact opposites; Robards was as quiet as a mouse, hardly saying a word. Telly told tall tales at the drop of a hat with the volume turned way up. I did three of those shows before they pulled the plug. Thank you, John Robinson!

In mid-1961 we purchased a home in North Hollywood and with that move my good fortune seemed to disappear. Oh, I continued to work but the pickings were sparse. I began to look around for another way to support my family. A friend of mine named Bud Doty went into real estate and he encouraged me. So I went to a real estate school and in October I passed my test and received my license. I went to the company where I had bought my house. The broker there, George Poppers, took me on.

Although 1961 had me doing shows, commercials and pictures, the monetary rewards did not keep pace with my family needs. Real estate sales income took up the slack and for the next ten years I had two sources of income: acting and real estate. It worked out pretty well. In 1961 I had a role in a motion picture entitled *Patty* (also called *Case of Patty Smith*). Believe it or not, I played a procurer for an abortionist, a very interesting role. I also did a half-dozen commercials and ten TV shows. And in the last three months of the year I made three sales and listed six properties. I wasn't making a living in real estate, but I was on my way.

1962 was the transition year. I moved from showbiz to real estate in a big way. I supported myself quite well in real estate and my sideline was film work. I only did four TV shows, two of which were episodes of *Mister Ed*. Another show was *The Dick Powell Show*, directed by Don Taylor and produced by Aaron Spelling. I did a few commercials also but the year was poor compared to my real estate income.

Mister Ed was the only TV show I did in 1963. However, I did several commercials that paid reasonably well. The real estate business continued to prosper. The two crafts kept food in the cupboard. But, on the day that I filmed the *Mister Ed*, a man named Joe Pacelli approached me and told me about a play that he was about to direct at the Glendale Center Theater. He wanted me to audition for a leading role.

My marriage was on the rocks and I was about to move out of my house to see if a trial separation would help. It occurred to me that the rehearsals and running of the play could keep me busy during a tough period.

Because the Glendale Center Theatre was non-union, I had to take an assumed name. I chose "Hubert R. Weiss," which was the name of the man who sold me our home. When the local Glendale newspaper reviewed the play the headline was "Hubert R. Weiss Steals the Show." I was kept busy and soon I had another offer. The Pasadena Playhouse was doing a 1940s musical entitled *Best Foot Forward*. A friend of mine, Kelton Garwood, had been cast in the role of the reporter. For some reason he had to cancel out and called me. He told me that he would recommend me to the director, Wes Kenny, if I was interested. The marriage separation needed more time so, once again, a play would keep me intelligently occupied. At least I would work using my own name and there was a small salary.

Ruth Burch, a very important casting director, contacted me in June and asked me if I would like to do a play at the quite prestigious La Jolla Playhouse. It starred Mike Connors whom I knew from Jeff Corey's class. It involved a ten-day rehearsal and a two-week run. La Jolla is a suburb of San Diego about two hours from Hollywood and I could use the vacation. I took it.

My commercial agent called me during the short run and had an interview for me. It turned out to be one of the most bizarre jobs I ever had. The product was Plymouth. While I sat in the waiting room at Paramount, a fellow actor was coming down the hall shaking his head and talking aloud. He kept saying over and over again, "They must be nuts. They want me to work with a fucking lion!!" He didn't stop at the desk to sign out, but continued right out the exit door. The secretary called my name and down the hall I went. When I reached the interview room, I faced about ten people. They were all bent over, still laughing their heads off at the last actor. I waited politely until one man regained his composure.

"This commercial would have you working with a lion. Would you work with a lion?"

I told them that I would. I then read the scene with the casting director. I was dismissed without further interaction.

Before I would get on the freeway and head for La Jolla, I called my agent. He said he was happy I called because he had another interview for me. (This was still before the day of cell phones or pagers.) The inter-

Jerry Colonna and I make plans to party on Dennis The Menace.

view was just a short ways away. When I got there, they explained that they were looking for a spokesman for a Midwest oil company. They had a video camera set up and recorded the scene. They thanked me and away I went to La Jolla. The next day my agent called and told me that I got both jobs.

On September 3 and 4 we shot the Plymouth commercial. The script called for me to be driving a new (1965) Plymouth convertible. The script had me driving up to an intersection and stopping at a red light. A truck, hauling a caged lion, pulls up next to me and stops. The driver of the truck asks me what kind of car I'm driving. I go into a spiel informing him of all the great features of the car. In the meantime, the lion nudges its cage open and hops into the backseat of the car. With that, the light changes and I take a left turn and drive down a street. Passersby on the street are yelling at me, telling me that there's a lion in the backseat of my car. Of course, I think they are all yelling in amazement at my beautiful new car. I answer the townspeople with proud lines such as, "Yeah, it's a new Plymouth, ain't she a beauty?" The car then turns right and heads up a steep hill. A printed statement appears superimposed over the departing car. The statement read, "Lion optional."

When I arrived on the set in Sierra Madre, just outside of Pasadena, the lion trainer was working with "Major," a 600-pound lion who had worked in Tarzan movies. The trainer was trying to get the lion to jump into the backseat of a Plymouth. He finally did it. The cat landed in the car and the entire front end of the car bounced up several feet. This was definitely not acceptable!

We shot the sequences where I have the conversation with the truck driver and then the director decided to shoot the scene where I'm driving down the street with the townspeople aghast at seeing the lion sitting up in the backseat. They wanted to get a close-up of me at the steering wheel with the lion's head behind and slightly above mine. It was a hot day and, in the sunlight, it was probably several degrees above 100. In one of the rehearsals Major opened up his huge mouth and roared just as the lion does at the opening of all the MGM movies. The roar just about deafened me. I stepped out of the car and said, "That's lunch or I'm going to be his."

The director laughed and asked me to get back in the car for another take. I told him no and went across the street where the caterer was setting up lunch. I told the director to take the lion to a shady spot and let him cool down. I was serious. I wasn't going to be his lunch.

The next day my line about my being the lion's lunch was quoted by Mike Connolly in his column in *The Hollywood Reporter*. What price celebrity?

The commercial went on to win a "Clio," which is the Oscar of the commercial world.

The commercials I did for John Forney Co. of Minneapolis were for Western Oil & Fuel and were both lucrative and interesting. My character was named Westy and the commercials were more like mini-commentaries. The association lasted two years and I did over thirty TV commercials and many radio spots.

I continued to work in real estate, but my heart was still in showbiz. I absolutely knew that one fine day a show would come along and rescue me from the workaday world. It was a strange dichotomy that kept me true to two masters. Although I loved showbiz, I didn't trust it. And although I enjoyed serving buyers and sellers, I rather resented the time the industry demanded. The balance of 1965 I did quite a few more commercials and only a few shows, including two more *Mister Eds*.

1966 turned out to be a landmark year in my life. I had been using Dr. Ron Berez for about four years as my personal physician. As we sat in his office going over results of tests, he suddenly stared at me and asked me if I had ever thought of surgery on my ears. I told him, no, and asked why. He told me that my ears stuck out and that there certainly would be more roles open to me if my ears did not protrude.

It was true, my ears did stick out but I had never thought about having cosmetic surgery. Dr. Berez told me that he had a doctor friend who did cosmetic surgery and that I should consider it. To make a long story short, I went to see Dr. Goldstone and he quoted me a very low price. The hospitalization would be covered by Blue Cross. He said that I would have bandages on my head for about a week. I decided to do it. I was living in a very small apartment in Sherman Oaks and stayed indoors for most of the recovery week.

A few weeks later I met the girl of my dreams. She was 23 and I was 38. Her name was Louise Teecher and she gave my life a new meaning. Life was more than just paying bills and taking care of mundane chores. I met her family and once again I believed in myself and a future.

I did a pilot film starring Carol Channing that was directed by Desi Arnaz. Lucille Ball was in the audience and so was Louise. I did a *Green Acres* that year also but real estate was in a real funk. Interest rates were up to 11%, which means that there were virtually no sales. Somehow I made it through the year. I did a few commercials, collected residuals and did a couple of TV shows like *Felony Squad* and *The Beverly Hillbillies*.

Louise and I became very close during this period in 1967. We had dinner together almost every night. I had my kids every other weekend and worked very hard in real estate. I joined a dynamic company by the name of Forest Olson, Realtors and listings and sales came my way as the interest rates improved. There was once again a real estate business. I prayed that showbiz would also bounce my way. That didn't occur, but there was some joy in life. Louise and I talked about marriage, but my life had to straighten out first.

We rolled into 1968 with my situation not changing much. I was still doing commercials, selling real estate and cashing residual checks. I managed to stay afloat. Showbiz had me doing only two TV shows, *The Good Guys* and the first of several *Bracken's World* shows.

1969 started with the worst event that I could ever imagine. My sainted mother died on January 17. I had moved her from Hawthorne to Van Nuys a year earlier so that I could be more help. Her heart was failing her. I was only two minutes away and was able to spend a lot of time with her. I took her to her doctor in Santa Monica weekly and had lunch with her at least once a week. We attended Mass every Sunday. Louise was a big help during Mom's last year, covering for me when business kept me from our regular times together. My mother's death was apparently painless. When I found her, she was in bed with her rosary entwined around both hands. She was a marvelous mother and I will never forget her love and understanding for me. She was 76. The Funeral Mass was at St. Jane Frances Church in Van Nuys and she was buried next to my father. It rained from the moment she died until she was buried three days later. I like to think that it was a mammoth show of tears at her death. God bless you, Mary Margaret McMahon Conley. You were absolutely the finest mother.

1969 would become a red-letter year even though it started on such a sad note. The crossover had materialized. Although I did a picture, *80 Steps to Jonah,* directed by my old friend, Gerd Oswald, there was very little other showbiz activity. A Plymouth commercial completed my acting year. Thank God for real estate. It provided the majority of my 1969 income.

CHAPTER THIRTEEN

A New Life!

To my great joy, Louise Ann Teecher agreed to marry me and on June 28, 1969 we said our vows. Her parents stood up for us and the ceremony was performed by a Unitarian minister, John Findly. He and his wife, Lillian, supplied their home for the ceremony. I had sold it to them a year or two earlier. There were only thirteen people in attendance. My family was represented by my niece, Gay. My sister was on a vacation trip which could not be cancelled on short notice. Louise's family made up most of the attendees. Jerry Hopper was there with his camera for a few shots.

We moved into a two-bedroom apartment in Sherman Oaks. It served us temporarily until we bought a home after only five months of marriage. It was a two-bedroom and den home in Granada Hills, in an area where I had been selling quite a few homes. I was able to use my GI Bill, which meant no down payment. I received a commission as the selling salesman which afforded us the opportunity to have the house painted and carpeted. We moved in on the weekend following Thanksgiving. We were doing all right!

Early 1970 found Louise and me settling into our marriage in our new home. Kevin and Julie visited with us on an irregular basis but Louise wanted her own children and I completely agreed. We also wanted to travel and a dream beckoned us. Through her teacher's organization we were able to get a chartered roundtrip flight to London for a very economical amount. Once babies came our way, an extended European trip would be out of the question. So in July we were off on a magical tour of Europe. Louise had been there before so she became my devoted tour guide.

Thirty days later we were back home and I began to investigate various plans which would put me in my own business. I had been selling homes for nine years, 1961- 1970. I definitely felt qualified. On December 10, 1970, I opened my own little office. I purchased four desks and chairs and put papers on each desk so it looked as if the office could be operational for four or more. One by one I took listings on homes. One by one, I sold houses. And, one by one, I hired salespeople. Believe it or not, by the middle of 1971, I was ready for one more change. A good corner location became available and I grabbed it. The space was at the corner of Woodman and Oxnard and came with a large electric sign which could be refaced easily.

At that point I became aware of a new concept: franchising. Red Carpet Realtors had just opened fourteen offices in the San Fernando Valley and, for a small fee, I could be the 15th office. Franchising suddenly made fifteen small independent offices look like a fifteen-office chain replete with a referral system, full-page ads, and an identity which would take a decade to build. I jumped on board with both feet and with the move from Burbank Blvd. to Woodman Ave. I also changed identities from an unknown "Joseph H. Conley, Realtor" to easily identifiable, "Red Carpet Realtors, Joseph H. Conley, Broker."

My sales staff, all clad in Red Blazers, were excited with the change. Business leaped forward and I was happy for another reason: Louise was pregnant with a late September or early October delivery date.

My showbiz activities slowed to a sickly stall. 1971 had me doing an industrial for I.T.T. and one commercial advertising Gerber's Baby Foods. Good timing on that one.

October 19, about two weeks late, Erin Elizabeth made her debut. She was gorgeous and so welcome. Grandmother Jean was there for the arrival. Louise spent four days in the hospital and then brought the most welcome baby home to her excited family. Louise left the teaching profession, never to return. Our home would be blessed for many years to come.

In late 1971 my office was doing so well that I was like a poster boy. From practically nothing, I took my infant company to the point where the office was full of salespeople and business could not have been better. Red Carpet was expanding and I wanted to be a part of it. I spoke with Del Wall, the VP in charge of expansion, and worked out a deal. I would make presentations three days a week to brokers in Orange County using my success story along with Red Carpet's sudden fantastic growth. In return I would be paid $1,000 a month and have the option to buy $2,500 in stock in Red Carpet Corporation. When Orange County was sold out my extra job was concluded. Red Carpet was now in several areas, San Francisco, Sacramento, San Fernando Valley, San Gabriel Valley, and Orange County. San Diego, Phoenix, Texas and Florida were in the near future. At this point I bought another franchise for North Hollywood. I still had to find a location.

CHAPTER FOURTEEN

Two Professions

The blending of the two professions was not difficult the first season. My contract with Lorimar Productions, the producers of *The Waltons*, called for me to appear in seven out of thirteen shows. Each show was scheduled to be filmed in six and a half days. I averaged about two days per show and most often I was only at the studio about four hours. Inasmuch as my office was only about fifteen minutes from the studio, I would often go into the real estate office first thing in the morning, go over to the studio at 11:00 A.M. and be back in the office by 3:00 P.M. Occasionally, I would be compelled to be at the studio from morning till night: 7:00 A.M. till 7:00 P.M. But that didn't occur very often. My office secretary, Maxine Gillihan, was under strict orders to never call me at the studio. On the other hand, there was a public phone just outside the studio door. I could call at anytime to take care of emergencies. The scripts were exceedingly well written and I was positive that the show would be picked up for the second thirteen shows.

The Waltons debuted on September 14, 1972 and was greeted with outstanding reviews. The show was different from anything else on TV. The creative process by actors, writers, and directors melded well. It was a foregone conclusion that the show would be picked up for a full year. Our ratings were superb, knocking *The Mod Squad* and *The Flip Wilson Show* for a loop. Both shows had been in the top ten the previous season.

As far as my real estate schedule was concerned, I worked six days a week, arriving at my office at around 10:00 A.M. and working until about 5:00 P.M. Most of my time was spent in management, but I still listed houses for sale when I received personal referrals. Buyers, however, I referred to salespeople based upon their production and enthusiasm. My staff filled all the desks in the office (12). Before long, either because of my management skills (?) or Red Carpet's obvious success, I had a full staff of competent salespeople. Success breeds success. In 1972 I was able to manage both professions with very little problems.

The atmosphere on Stage 26 at The Burbank Studios: *The Waltons* set was, for the most part, congenial and very friendly. Whenever I arrived on the set I received smiles and warm greetings. During any filming, no matter the show, when one enters a soundstage, he is immediately aware that one area on the stage is lit up. The rest of the space is dimly lit. The film crew and actors are either filming or rehearsing, or the set is being lighted and dressed. There are usually a few people, other than the cast and crew, who stand and watch.

On *The Waltons* set there was a group of eight or ten people who usually sat in a circle and conversed quietly until "Quiet on the set!" was requested by the assistant director. This group was the parents of the Walton kids. The kids, three boys and three girls, were aged seven to seventeen: Kami Cotler, 7; David Harper, 10; Mary McDonough, 11; Eric Scott, 12; Judy Taylor, 15, and Jon Walmsley, 17. The circle-sitting group was parents, almost always mothers. They were legally required to be there by the Coogan Law, which, presumably, guaranteed that minors were looked after. Without exception, these parents were wonderful. The kids, during the shooting year, were in a one-room schoolhouse (a huge trailer, really) just outside the stage. There, they were tutored five days a week. They were allowed to work only four hours a day, between the hours of 9:00 A.M. until 6:00 P.M. There were no exceptions to these rules. The teacher and parents were there to make sure the rules were followed. You can imagine that this complicated the filming process where long hours are the rule rather than the exception. The kids were all good kids. They laughed and played, as children will do, but when "serious time" arrived they were mindful of the filming process. One kid, Eric Scott, was funny. He was old beyond his years and a complete cut-up. Once again, though, he knew when to fool around and when to be mindful of time constraints. I'll talk more about Eric later.

The adults on the show were Richard Thomas (John-Boy), Michael Learned (Olivia Walton), Ralph Waite (John Walton), Will Geer (Grandpa Walton), and Ellen Corby (Grandma Walton). John Crawford was a regular the first season, playing the Sheriff. His role was not used much the first year and he became what is known as an "in-and-out regular." Emily and Mamie Baldwin (Mary Jackson and Helen Kleeb) were in that category also. Allow me to introduce each of these as they appeared to me during the initial season.

I described Richard Thomas as an actor with the enthusiasm of an eleven-year-old and the consummate skill of a fifty-year-old. He had a photographic memory and an innate sense of humor. I had many scenes with him and he was thoroughly professional when the camera was turning and professionally humorous between takes. He was, and is, one smart young man.

Michael Learned was a consummate actor who made no bones about her love for the theatre and her distain of film and television. She was always pleasant and prepared but the joy of acting was reserved for the stage.

Ralph Waite is a fine actor who kept to himself most of the time. He directed some shows and had ambitions to produce and star in films. During our off-season (hiatus) one year, he wrote, produced, funded, and starred in a film entitled *On the Nickel*. It had limited success. When *The Waltons* ended, he co-produced and starred in his own series entitled *The Mississippi*. It had some success and ran for a couple of seasons. In *Roots*, the renowned miniseries, he brilliantly played the slave ship captain.

Will Geer was seventy when the show started and had been a professional actor for more than forty-five years. He was blacklisted during the McCarthy era when he refused to "name names" about people he knew to have communist leanings. He only worked sporadically as a professional actor for over ten years. He played Broadway, toured, owned a Shakespeare Company and had his own theatre in Topanga Canyon, a semi-hippy mountainous community adjacent to Los Angeles. He had many children and loved to introduce his most recent ex-wife as "my favorite ex-wife." He had absolutely no inhibitions but, in his own way, was quiet and unobtrusive. I went to lunch with him many times and loved to get him telling stories of his escapades. One observation I had was that in rehearsals he was physically bent over and soft-spoken. But when the camera was rolling in a "take" he stretched himself to his full 6'2" and spoke his dialogue in stentorian tones that would shake the rafters. He, along with Richard Thomas, Michael Learned and Ellen Corby, won Emmys for their performances on *The Waltons*.

Ellen Corby, who had played supporting roles in pictures and TV for over forty years, was a delightful lady. For some unknown reason she took a liking for me and, on several occasions, called for me to come and join the group for publicity photos. I remember one time she advised me to be at the Walton house at 2:00 P.M. "They're going to do a publicity shot of the family. You should be there, too." I was there, as she advised. She invited me to join the group for one of the photos. That's a photo that I still enjoy today.

John Crawford is about my age and, like me, had played supporting roles in pictures and TV for years. He was also a writer and a musician. He played a mean guitar. The Sheriff's appearances occurred when problems arose in a story and an official was needed to straighten things out. Unfortunately for him, most of the scripts had little innocent problems which were attended to by family or friends. The Baldwin sisters, Emily and Mamie, who made moonshine but thought it was medicine, filled a comedy slot that was silly and fun. Mary Jackson and Helen Kleeb were perfect in their roles. I laugh today when I think of some of the silly situations the sisters and their "recipe" got into.

Many people are not aware of the fact that John Ritter (*Three's Company*) appeared on *The Waltons* several times. He played the Baptist Minister, Rev. Fordwick. The Rev. Fordwick was anything but typical. In his first appearance he got wildly drunk on the "recipe." When he was on the show, it was fun time. He and Richard Thomas were a delight to watch as they attempted to outdo each other in silliness and comedic bits. They out-drooled each other. It was obvious to those of us who worked with him that it was just a matter of time before he would score his own triumph either in a motion picture or on TV. He was loaded with talent and was a joy to work with.

The first season of the series consisted of twenty-five hours of film. We started with a contract from CBS to do thirteen hours which was extended when our ratings went through the roof. I had been guaranteed seven out of thirteen shows and wound up doing exactly that, 13 of 25.

Some of the finest writers in Hollywood wrote scripts that season. I'll name a few: Earl Hamner (the creator), William Bast, Nigel McKeand, Paul Savage, William Welch, John Furia and John McGreevey. McGreevey later won the Emmy with his script, "The Scholar" in that first season.

I worked a total of thirty-five days for those thirteen shows in which I appeared. Some of the shows I had just one scene while others (two) I worked as many as five days.

In early December I was called at home and asked to come to the set. A magazine was doing a spread on the store. I was surprised to discover that it was *TV Guide*. Two weeks later when the magazine hit the news-stands I saw that the whole country knew who "Ike" was and who played the role. It was a real plum.

The show's ratings made it to the top. We were rated first in the nation of prime-time television shows. I felt very grateful.

We went on hiatus in early March of 1973, absolutely sure that there would be at least one more year of *The Waltons*. Most of us felt that the show could be a long-running series.

I've already spoken about the quality of our scripts. Earl Hamner, the creator of *The Waltons*, knew exactly what he wanted and made sure that each script could have happened. He and the producers also knew exactly the kind of person who would run the show on the set: the direc-tor. They chose men (and women) who were quality people themselves like Harry Harris, Jack Shea, Vince Sherman, Phil Leacock, Ralph Sen-ensky, Alf Kjellin and Bob Butler. Many of these directors I had worked with before in other shows dating back to the fifties. In most cases it was like old home week. I was so friendly with Jack Shea that when it came time for Erin to be baptized we chose Pat and Jack Shea.

My personal choices for the best shows of that first season included John McGreevey's "The Foundling," Earl Hamner's "The Fire," and Paul Savage's "The Dust Bowl Cousins."

For Louise and me, we had all sorts of thankfulness. Our baby, Erin Elizabeth, was well into her second healthy year. Red Carpet was doing extremely well and the future looked bright.

CHAPTER FIFTEEN

The Second Season

The Waltons' second season coincided with the opening of our second Red Carpet office. I was blessed by being able to convince Mike Charles to come out of retirement and manage the new office in North Hollywood. Mike was a quality guy who helped make our second office as productive as our first one in a very short time.

Things were moving very fast for us at that time. One of the things we were attempting to do was to move to a larger home. Louise and I had been looking all during the spring and early summer of 1973. I had an opportunity to join some Red Carpet realtors from Phoenix, Sacramento, San Francisco and the San Gabriel Valley in a camping trip up in the High Sierras. I had never done anything like that before and it was thrilling. The trip would be completed just before we would start shooting the second season. We horse packed out of the little town of Independence in the Owens Valley up the steep eastern slopes of the Sierras. Then we camped out, fished for trout and lived the outdoors life as the cowboys set up our camp, prepared our meals and guided us around one of nature's most beautiful areas. When the five-day trip ended, I got in my car and headed home. I stopped along the road and called home. Louise assured me that everything was fine and I told her I'd see her in a couple of hours. I reached home at about 5:30 and, after hugging Louise and Erin, I asked what was new. Without answering, she opened the refrigerator door and withdrew a frosty pitcher of martinis. She poured and then answered my question about what was new.

"I bought a new house," she said with no more excitement in her voice than I would expect if she had told me that she bought a loaf of bread.

I said, "What?"

She repeated her statement and then I asked why she didn't tell me when I called a couple of hours earlier.

"I wanted to wait until you had a martini in front of you."

We laughed, clinked our glasses and then she began to tell me about the new house. It was bigger, it had a pool, it was relatively new (seven years new), and had four bedrooms. I wanted to see it and she informed me that we had an appointment in fifteen minutes.

"Do I have to sign the agreement tonight?" I asked.

"No, you don't have to sign anything. I forged your name."

I sipped my martini and accepted the fact of who wore the pants in my household.

I checked the house out and it was perfect. The cost was well within our budget and the size would be perfect for us. The neighborhood was lovely and I could find nothing to complain about. The next day I went to work on *The Waltons*, which was a lot more calm than life at home with a new office, a new baby, a new home and an exciting wife.

My two professions were separate and unique. I tried my best to keep them that way, but occasionally they would cross. In the early fall of 1973 an interesting set of circumstances occurred. I got a call from an old customer. I had sold him and his bride a home a couple years previously when I was working with Forrest Olson Realtors. He called me with an odd request. He told me about a house in Van Nuys that his wife had seen and wanted to buy. He gave me a phone number of the owner and the address of the property.

"The house isn't listed. I want you to list it and I'll buy it. Then you can list my house and sell that also. I called them and they're expecting you tonight at 7:30."

It was Thursday and I usually kept that time open so Louise and I could watch *The Waltons*. But we were talking about a lot of money, maybe a couple of thousand dollars. The show that night was a rerun. So, at the appointed time, I rang the doorbell. The husband and wife greeted me rather coolly. I took a tour through the house, and then glanced at the yard. I then presented them with a list of comparable sales in the immediate area. I had done my homework. Suddenly, the couple got in a furious fight about things that had nothing to do with me. The argument went on for a few minutes. Then there was a pause in the quarrel and I jumped in. I presented them with a couple of my business cards and told them to call me when they were ready to talk business. The husband yelled, "No, we're gonna work this out tonight. You stay here. We'll go in the den and settle this."

He and his wife left the room and, a minute later, a boy, of about ten, entered the living room and closed the door to the den behind him. The boy looked at me and flashed a perfunctory smile. He pointed at the TV and asked me if he could turn it on. I smiled and told him it was okay by me. As the set warmed up, he changed channels until he found CBS. The familiar theme music of *The Waltons* sang sweetly from the set. The boy seated himself on the floor immediately in front of the set. After the standard opening, the show began at Ike Godsey's store. John Boy was just finishing pumping some gas in the family truck. Ike was sitting on a box in front of the store, painting an old bicycle a bright blue. It was an episode entitled "The Bicycle." As Ike and John Boy engaged in some opening banter, the boy turned around and looked at me, then back to the screen, then back to me, then back to the screen. He took one more studied appraisal of me, then dashed through the den door yelling for his mommy and daddy. I continued watching the show until the boy reentered the room from the den. He was dragging his father in front of the set. The wife followed. The boy pointed at me, then the TV. "He's Ike Godsey on *The Waltons*." During the ensuing minutes the story had progressed and, at that moment, there was a scene between John and Olivia Walton.

They all studied the screen for a few moments. "He ain't on the show," said the father.

The boy knew better and he insisted. "He isn't on the show now, but he was and he'll be back."

The father was going to settle the matter. He looked at me and asked, "You aren't on the show, are ya?"

Before I could answer, the show progressed and Olivia entered the store and started a conversation with Ike. The four of us watched the scene play as Ike tried to sell Olivia the bike. He then encouraged her to take it for a trial spin. She acquiesced, got on the bike and wobbled out of the scene.

The family was entranced by what they had just seen and when the commercial came on, they all had questions. I assured them that I was a full-time real estate broker who moonlighted as an actor. When the commercial ended we all watched the show until its completion. A half hour later I had listed the house. When I left the family, they were all smiling. Ike Godsey had served as a marriage counselor. And, by the way, I made the sale and listed the other home. Everything was working.

In September of 1973 *The Waltons* just about swept the Emmy Awards. The show won Best Dramatic Series. Richard Thomas and Michael Learned won Best Actors. Ellen Corby won Best Supporting Actor. Lee Philips won Best Director and John McGreevey won Best Writer. The show was going to be around for awhile.

The second season had me in 18 of the 24 shows filmed. I was at the studio only 35 days, which left plenty of time for me to run the company. However, since the show was a big success, it was only natural that the actors would be asking for more money. I acquiesced to that thought process myself. However, I did not have an agent and would have to do it myself. I called Lee Rich, the executive producer, and he took my call but told me that he was too busy to spend time with me. He told me to call Neil Mafeo who was a vice president of Lorimar Productions. When I called Neil, he readily accepted my invitation to have lunch. Neil was a very nice man and a good friend of Jack Shea's. He listened politely to my pitch for an increase in salary. When I completed my proposal, Neil told me, with all the honesty that he could muster, that it was his job to get my services at the cheapest possible price. I was dealing with a pro and I was an amateur. He did get back to me a couple weeks later. He told me that he could offer me a raise if I would agree to two more years on my contract. It would be a trade-off. I get more money and the company gets more time. I agreed. The shooting season of 1973-74 finished with pleasant feelings all around. The show, per the Nielsen ratings, hung in there, week after week, in the #1, #2 or #3 positions.

My real estate company continued to do well. And I decided to expand my operation to include escrow and insurance. I had an opportunity to rent a small office building which would be a private office for me and a headquarters for the two offices. I hired a manager for the Van Nuys office and an escrow officer. Business was good and it was prudent for me to expand the services. I still didn't trust showbiz. Although I had seven years to go on my contract, it was at *The Waltons* annual option. My real estate company would go on as long as I "watched the store."

In June of '74 the third season of *The Waltons* began and the option for my services was picked up by the producers. But there was a change. John Boy (Richard Thomas) was going off to college. The scripts had large portions taking place away from Walton's Mountain and the family. In about half of the shows Ike Godsey was not in the cast. The producers left the door open, however, by having John Boy get a car (a yellow Model A with a rumble seat). He was a day student, driving daily from home to school and back. I believe the producers were watching very carefully to see if the ratings changed or if the mail voiced a non-acceptance to the change from Walton's Mountain to Boatright College.

Along about November 1, the producers invited me over to the office for a little meeting and surprised me by informing me that Ike Godsey was about to have a wife. They gave me a copy of the script entitled "The Matchmakers." I was also notified that they were holding interviews for my screen wife in a few days. I volunteered to read with the interviewees, but they said that was not necessary. I took the script home and shared the news with Louise that I was about to have a second wife. We both enjoyed reading the script and it certainly looked as if Ike's role was being enlarged. The story resembled the script on *The People's Choice* (the Jackie Cooper show) of twenty years earlier. The script had Corabeth Walton, a distant cousin of John's, suddenly show up at their doorstep and move in. It seems that her family had died off and the family house was lost to the bankers. However, the spinster was a troublemaker and a thorn in the side of the Walton house. It was decided to try to marry her off to Ike. After all, Ike needed a wife, and Corabeth needed a home, particularly away from the Walton house. The script, written by John McGreevey, was a gem, full of humor and pathos.

A few days later Bob Jacks, the producer, appeared on the set and introduced me to Ronnie Claire Edwards who had been selected to be the new Mrs. Godsey. The meeting was most pleasant. I complimented her on getting the role and she expressed her delight at getting the chance to appear on her favorite show. I invited her to lunch and, in addition to reading a few of the scenes we had together, we learned about each other. I was surprised to learn that she presently lived in New York. Her agent in New York learned about the role being cast and secured the interview for her. She paid her own way to Hollywood for the interview. Ronnie Claire grew up in Oklahoma and lived for many years in Texas. She naturally had a country accent which fit right in with the show. She was a lovely looking young lady about five years younger than I. She had never done any television, but she had just finished doing a film which had been shot on location in Kansas. Her experience before that had been working on the stage in theaters in and around Dallas. She surprised me by being very complimentary about my masculinity. It seems that working in regional theater, she was very often paired up with leading men who weren't too manly.

In 1974, Ike married Corabeth Walton (Ronnie Claire Edwards), a cousin of the Waltons. The writers made it a marriage not made in heaven.

The cast of *The Waltons* warmed to her immediately. She was talented and funny. Everybody enjoyed working with her. When we finished filming that episode, she retuned to New York.

"The Matchmakers" aired on January 9, 1975. It was reviewed in *Daily Variety* and the reviewer was generous in his compliments of Ronnie Claire and me, along with John McGreevey's script. At the end of the season Ronnie Claire was brought out to Hollywood to do a couple more shows, but there was no word about her becoming a regular.

The third season of *The Waltons* ended on a warm, most pleasant note. The series was doing well, the real estate offices were rolling along and Louise and I were about to enlarge the size of our family. On May 22 Jana Lynne was born. At eight pounds, she was a lovely little girl who was welcomed with open arms. My in-laws, Jean and Bel Teecher, had returned to L.A. from the San Francisco Bay area. So the newborn not only had devoted parents but loving grandparents as well. When the fourth season of *The Waltons* began, there was no Corabeth in sight. I asked the producers and the answer was in the negative. They had offered her a contract but she refused to sign it. It seems that she had written a play and it was being produced and she didn't wish to leave New York for an extended time. My next question was an obvious one: My character is married to a person who is not there. How was that going to be handled? I was told that for the time being that they would "dance" around her non-presence. My character would say that she's feeling poorly, she's visiting relatives, she'll be back in a little while…etc. I was told that they were trying to work something out so that she could come west for a couple of shows. I didn't particularly like the situation. It occurred to me that Ronnie Clair's absence would undoubtedly influence Ike's participation. But there was nothing I could do.

The cast of The Waltons *and I in about 1975.*

CHAPTER SIXTEEN

The Busiest Year

If you were to ask me at the time if all the things that happened in that year could have occurred I would have told you "no way."

First and foremost, Ronnie Claire Edwards signed a contract which then freed the writers so that they could write for The Godseys. The first script of the season, "The First Edition," written by John McGreevey, blended two stories. The main plot concerned the publishing of the first edition of the *Blue Ridge Chronicle*, John Boy's newspaper. The secondary plot wound itself around Ike and Corabeth's excitement of becoming parents only to be dashed when the truth revealed a false pregnancy.

A few weeks later, the Godseys told everyone in Walton's Mountain that they were about to adopt a baby. This enthusiasm blended with the major plot which had Jim-Bob (David Harper) engaged in "The Great Motorcycle Race." Jim-Bob's motorcycle was Ike's with the sidecar removed. The two stories mixed well. Jim-Bob finished third and Ike and Corabeth adopted a ten-year-old, Aimee Louise. Aimee became Elizabeth's best friend and the Godseys became the second family on Walton's Mountain.

Inasmuch as there were many young people on the show, they began to grow up with the calendar. Each year the kids were a year older and so was I. It was the first television show that I was aware of that moved forward each year with the calendar. This became obvious particularly as the Second World War loomed on the horizon and then arrived. The producers took the liberty to move two years ahead on one occasion.

In early 1976 I spoke with Jon Walmsley, who played Jason Walton, about the possibility of putting together a song-and-dance act that would work the County and State Fairs. He was very polite but turned me down. He had plans to move forward on his own. I thanked him and then thought of Eric Scott. I approached him with the same general plan and

Eric Scott and I on The Waltons and also in our song and dance act.

he was openly enthusiastic. I asked him if he could sing. He answered
with a phrase that endeared me to him. He said, "I haven't but I think I
can." I put him together with a voice coach that I knew and the report
came back that he didn't have a "big voice" like I did but he could carry a
tune and, with amplification, he'd be fine. A friend of mine, by the name

of Don Ralke, was very enthused and wanted to be a part of it and, later in the year, Eric, Don and I would get together a couple times a week and knock around ideas and songs. Eric and I paid Don hourly for his input, which was considerable. His background of recording, songwriting, and continuity blended well with our enthusiasm without actual experience. We'd meet at Don's house in Sherman Oaks in the morning. Our conversation would very often carry into the afternoon. We'd go to a nearby hotel for lunch. Eric and I would flip a coin for the tab and we've continued the habit until the present time. I think I'm ahead!

In March, Louise and I appeared on *Tattle Tales* and Louise, for the first time in her life, received a check for her appearance. We shot five shows in one day. Our friends and relatives got to see Louise as a performer. She did fine!

Early that year I made a decision which worked out and didn't work out. I'll explain. My two offices in North Hollywood and Van Nuys were doing well. I had a manager at each office on salary and I had a headquarters office which handled training, escrow and insurance. When the opportunity arose for me to open a third office in Northridge, the community where we lived, I jumped at it, feeling that I had the business structure which could easily handle another office. The owner of that franchise, Ray Rech, had quit the program. So there I was, the owner of a new franchise, but I didn't even have a location. I advertised for a manager and in a week or so, I had my man. I put him on salary. His sole responsibility in the beginning was to find a suitable location in the Northridge area. After a couple of weeks passed, he was frustrated that he couldn't come up with a good location. But I told him to keep digging. There had to be something, even if it were a temporary location.

On St. Patrick's Day, March 17, a Thursday, I attended my Toastmaster meeting in the AM and had a lot of fun leading all my Jewish friends in an Irish songfest. I went to a St. Pat's Day luncheon and sang and then headed home. As I passed Ray Rech's office, the former Red Carpet office, I decided, on the spur of the moment, to drop in for a friendly visit. He was seated at one of his desks and I broke into song as soon as I saw him. I regaled him with "The Kerry Dancers." He enjoyed the fun of my spur-of-the-moment appearance and applauded my effort. I then sat down and had a visit. While I was there, I asked him if he knew of a location where I could open an office. He got a strange look in his eye and then he asked me if I wanted his location. He was serious! He wanted out of the business for personal reasons and there it was: 2,400 square feet in a great location on a main boulevard and it had red carpeting.

The next day I brought Louise to help me make decisions and she agreed. I bought him out: furniture, red carpeting, lease, salespeople and all. A week later I was in business and Ray was on his way to Minnesota. I didn't know it at the time but the lease I was to assume was unusual in that it had six years to go and was at $.30 a square foot. The rent was way below market; an outright steal. The terms of the lease allowed the lessee (Ray Rech) to assign the lease provided the lessor (a Mr. Chazan) approved the financial statement of the new lessee (me). The phrase used in the lease assumption was that Mr. Chazan could not "unreasonably withhold" his permission. My accountant put together a Profit and Loss statement that honestly showed us in a very good light. In my meeting with Mr. Chazan, he expressed his willingness to sell the building and I was certainly interested, but it never occurred to me that it could happen.

Late in the shooting year the entire company was shocked to hear that Ellen Corby (Grandma Walton) had suffered a stroke. How serious it would be was unknown. For the time being, the writers wrote around her as they had done with Corabeth a year earlier. Later on we discovered that her condition prohibited her from speaking other than a few words. But she understood and comprehended everything around her. She would visit the set once in awhile. I remember one phrase she spoke over and over. It was "Oh boy!" The stroke was a tragedy for someone like Ellen who was so vital in real life and on the screen.

April through mid-June I was busy with three offices, three managers, hiring and training salespeople. Then, suddenly, it happened: all three managers departed. One I fired, one quit, and one was seriously ill. I was suddenly managing all three offices and *The Waltons'* season started. I was at the studio almost every day and some days the whole day. To use an old saying, "I was meeting myself coming home." Something had to give and I couldn't do anything about *The Waltons*. The show was red hot and, obviously, was going to run for years. Louise and I talked and came to the conclusion that I had bitten off more than I could chew. I told Louise that I believed that I could sell my two original offices in North Hollywood and Van Nuys. We decided to sleep on the decision and see how we felt in the morning.

The situation hadn't changed by morning and we decided to test the waters. I made a few phone calls and within a few days I had sold the two offices to the Millers. Jennie Miller bought the N. Hollywood, location and Ruth Miller bought the Van Nuys location. Some particulars had to be worked out, but on August 1 the transfer took place and I was down to one office. The manager who had been ill was well and I made him manager of the Northridge office. I was free to act and the Northridge office was on its way. Whew!!

One Sunday in February of 1976, I was driving the family home from church and Louise saw a sign which offered "Tennis On Your Lot" on a development in Chatsworth. "Let's go look at the model houses!" suggested Louise. My answer to her was that I looked at houses all the time. On my day off I didn't want to do that. "I went to church with you," Louise bargained. She was not religious and she was correct; she had attended Mass with us.

I agreed and in a few minutes we had viewed the three model homes. One was a single story which impressed Louise. A few days later our signatures were on the line and we looked forward to moving into a new home in July. Little did I know what would occur during the next few months. Within a relatively short time we would have our own home with a tennis court! The actual move-in occurred just a few weeks after we sold the offices. What a year that was.

CHAPTER SEVENTEEN

The Sixth Season

The sixth season started without our star. Richard Thomas had completed his five years, which was his contract. But the show was still hot and had to continue with or without him. I remember hearing the exaggeration that Richard had been offered North and South Dakota and half of Montana if he would return for another year but he wouldn't bite. He put it simply, "I'm twenty-six years old now and I want to begin playing mature men." I paraphrase but those are close to the words that he said to me.

There was also intrigue in that calendar year. I had been offered the lead role in a play at a theater called Tiffany's Attic in Salt Lake City. The play was *Send Me No Flowers*. The movie had starred Rock Hudson. The salary was acceptable but, more than that, playing that kind of a role would be good for my career. It was to run six weeks with one week of rehearsal. Louise couldn't accompany me for two important reasons. Jana, aged ten months, was too young to travel. With moving to the new house in July there were many decisions to be made. So it was agreed that I would do the play and Louise would keep the home fires burning for the seven weeks.

I left for Salt Lake City in the morning and drove until dark and spent the night in St. George in southern Utah. After breakfast in the morning, I completed the drive by late afternoon and checked into a motel, had dinner and settled into my room with all the local papers. I thought I would familiarize myself with the town and its happenings. In the morning, after breakfast, I reported in to the theater at 10:00 A.M. for the first meeting. I was surprised to see firemen and policemen all over the place. It was obvious by the odors that there had been a fire. I found the producer. He was quite rattled, as could be expected. He informed me that, for the time being, the production was postponed. He suggested that I return home; he would be in touch as soon as some major questions were answered. I stayed around for the balance of the day and that night I attended a show, *Four Poster*, starring Ken Berry, with whom I had worked years earlier when I sang with Horace Heidt. He told me that there were rumors about Tiffany's Attic. The production company was thought to be in financial trouble. And Richard Roundtree, the star of the current play, *Purlie Victorious*, had received some death threats. He was a black actor and some people in Salt Lake City didn't like a black starring in a play there. I contacted Actor's Equity, of which I was a member. They informed me that, in the event of a cancellation, I was to be paid two weeks salary. There was supposed to be a bond posted which would pay me. I never received a dime, including the cost of the motel, my meals and transportation. There were lots of things for me to do at home and I was welcomed there after a four-day experience. Strangely, this wasn't the end of the Salt Lake story. I'll pick up this story in a couple of years.

Later on, I was to negotiate with Mr. Chazan and bought the building on Reseda Blvd. I got an excellent buy and the building showed a profit from the very first day. Some things work out and some don't. We were to live happily in our Chatsworth house for fifteen years. You might wonder why I called it the Chatsworth house. Legally, the lot was in two communities. The house and address were in Chatsworth and the tennis court was in Northridge. Actually, we lived in Los Angeles. The names Chatsworth and Northridge referred to local post office designations.

At the completion of each year's shooting, the production company, Lorimar, would have what was known as a wrap party. Drinks and dinner were served. Sometimes the party was on a soundstage and at other times at a restaurant. In the spring of 1978 the party was held at Chasen's, a well-known Los Angeles restaurant. Louise and I left Chatsworth and allowed an hour for travel time, but on that day traffic was light and we were the first to arrive at 6:00 P.M. A few minutes later our executive producer, Lee Rich, arrived. He headed directly to us. We were the only guests in attendance. He greeted us enthusiastically and hugged each of us. He shouted, "Louise baby!" and "Joe baby," and congratulated us on contributing to another successful season. Lorimar was growing by leaps and bounds and I had a question for him regarding the expansion. "I understand you have a new show for next season, *Dallas*?"

He smiled and winked and stated the following, "That's right. Joe, the people want shit? Give it to 'em." That is an exact quote.

That spring, Eric Scott and I really got going on the act. We agreed on the theme which would be Ike sticking to the past, the golden oldies, while Eric countered with new music, the Beatles, etc. The dialogue during the show came easily to us once we settled on the music. So we had the music and the chatter but we had no idea of what to do to make it a song-and-dance act. Neither one of us knew anything beyond simple ballroom steps. We went through three choreographers until we finally located a guy who could teach us simple steps that appeared more sophisticated than they really were. Now it came time to break in the act. We did a half-dozen shows that allowed us to do the entire act, which at that time was close to an hour long. We went to San Diego and performed at the Red Carpet convention. We accompanied Ralph Edwards on his annual trek to Truth Or Consequences, NM. We performed for my Toastmasters club at their installation dinner and we did an afternoon show in the new auditorium at St. Jude's Church in Thousand Oaks. We also journeyed to Akron, Ohio, where we performed as part of the celebration of the National Soap Box Derby. We felt we were ready. So we took the advice of our manager, Jerry Wheeler, and did our act in Palm Springs for producers of fairs and exhibitions all over the country. And it worked! We got offers to do our act at the Wyoming County Fair in Grand Rapids, Michigan, the Multnoma Fair in Portland, Oregon and then another job at the California State Fair in Sacramento. That was the best job of all because the contract was for three days and then we got held over for three additional days.

We then got an opportunity to do *The Dinah Shore Show*, which was live on CBS. Later that year one of *The Waltons* scripts had Ike and Ben organizing a show for the servicemen in a nearby army camp. We took a small portion of the act and sang and danced as our characters in the show.

The spring of 1978 brought news of the most unpleasant kind. Will Geer had a stroke while traveling in Central America and died a week or so later. He was going to be sorely missed. He was such a warm, wonderful person who really enjoyed life and acting. News came my way from Salt Lake City. New producers of an entirely different company contacted me and wanted me to do *Send Me No Flowers*, once again playing the lead. I accepted the very generous offer, which included first-class air tickets for me and my family, a two-bedroom condo for the run of the play and an automobile for our use. The time was short, but I accepted the offer.

I flew to Salt Lake on the first of March and Louise and the girls (now three and six years old) were to follow ten days later. However, the job was not to be without some drama and I'm not talking about on the stage. The first day of rehearsal found me with a terrible cold or perhaps the flu. For a week I walked around with a Kleenex box in my hand along with the script. I was afraid to take medicine because it would affect my ability to memorize. The other actors were fearful that they would catch whatever I had. I was scared to death that I'd embarrass myself by blowing lines on stage. (And I'm sure the producers were fearful also.) But, somehow, I put it together and made it. I was line-perfect in the final dress rehearsal. Opening night was successful, also. I'm sure that those first few days of the production were not the best performances I ever gave, but, by the time my family arrived, I was healthy again. The show got good reviews and the six weeks in Salt Lake were really enjoyable. We skied. We took in all the sights in the area and the girls enjoyed their own activities also. Jana attended her first preschool, called Rocky Mountain Preschool. Erin enrolled in first grade at the local public school. I would walk her to school in the morning. Sometimes it was snowing, which was really exciting for her. Being from Buffalo, New York, snow didn't exactly thrill me. The development where our condo was located was called "Old Farm" and included a tennis facility which was inside a big balloon. We enjoyed that also.

One day when I was doing laundry, I was sitting there waiting for the dryer to do its job when a young man approached me and inquired if I was Ike Godsey on *The Waltons*. I told him I was and he surprised me by asking if I would do a commercial for a local company. I gave him my agent's name and phone number and told him to work it out. A few days later I did a commercial for a local bank. That was one of the most unusual jobs I ever got. One week I flew to L.A. on my day off (Monday) and recorded the entire song-and-dance act for a small record company. Eric and I each received quite a few copies as part of our contract. I still play it once in a while. It brings back memories.

When I returned home in mid-April, I was delighted to discover that I had a buyer for my Northridge Red Carpet office. I wouldn't make any money on the deal but I did get most of my investment back and a good tenant in my building.

The first show of the new season was entitled "The Empty Nest," written by Claire Whitaker and Rod Peterson. It said goodbye to the character of Grandpa Walton as portrayed by Will Geer.

Three of the five stars of the show were gone. Richard Thomas had retired and moved on. Ellen Corby, although physically available, was limited due to her inability to speak. Will Geer had passed on. But the show was still in the top ten and CBS wanted more. That meant that the Godseys would be used more and more and the Walton kids would get opportunities as the scripts moved on to World War II. My salary moved up and my contract called for me to appear in all of the shows. *The Waltons* now moved from rural Virginia to the world with events affecting the country and its citizens. I quote the scriptwriter John McGreevey and the words he used in the "The Illusion," which he wrote in July of 1978. These are the words of John-Boy as a man: "In these anxious and uncertain days when the rest of the world seemed to be fragmenting and collapsing under the assault of the Axis powers, my family and our friends and neighbors were questioning values, reassessing the attitudes and illusions that had sustained us in the past. Under stress, new insights were revealed." These words expressed the thoughts and dreams of the characters who peopled *The Waltons* scripts. I was most fortunate to be the recipient of thoughtful stories that could have happened.

In May of '78 Louise's mother, Jean, offered to baby sit the kids while Louise and I spent a lovely vacation in Hawaii; a week in Honolulu and a week in Maui. We spent Mother's Day as the guest of some *Waltons* fans at the Waikiki C.C. — really wonderful. Then we flew to Maui. Louise wasn't playing golf in those years, so I signed up for golf while Louise would take to the pool. The pro shop set me up to play with another guest of the hotel. His name was Paul Tebb from Gig Harbor (Tacoma), Washington. He was a delightful guy and we hit it off immediately. He was a big guy, about 6'4" or 6'5" and looked enough like Rock Hudson to be his twin. He bragged about his wife and I boasted my great fortune to have Louise at my side. Finishing golf, we both headed back to the hotel where we were to collect our spouses and have lunch together. When we went looking, we found them at the pool about fifteen feet from each other. We lunched together and then were virtually inseparable for the next five days. Pat Tebb had been a novice in a convent for a year or two. Her stories with herself as the butt of the joke were hilarious. It was clear to me that we would be friends for life. The sad tale is that Paul was killed in a head-on collision about eight months later. I remember being very upset over his death even though I only knew him for a few days in Hawaii. He was such a good guy with two young boys who needed a father. I prayed to God that I would be allowed to participate in the rearing of our two girls. Pat Tebb and her two boys came to visit us in San Clemente. But I'm getting ahead of my story.

CHAPTER EIGHTEEN

The Seventh Season

The first show of the new season was a two-hour episode and was dedicated to Will. As the year moved forward it was joy to read each succeeding script as Ike and Corabeth were more and more important to the story. The big thrill was to read "The Attack," which was Ike Godsey's heart attack. It was an odd feeling to play yourself having a serious health problem. Ike Godsey and Joe Conley were almost interchangeable. Ernie Wallengren wrote the episode. He had the thoughtfulness to spend some time with me before he wrote it asking many questions. Ernie was the son of our story editor, Claire Whitaker. The script was wonderful.

In our personal life Erin turned seven and Jana four. We determined that it would be wonderful to have a beach house at this age. So we began looking at houses from San Clemente south to La Jolla. In December we found a house in San Clemente. It was one hundred miles from Northridge. We made the deal and the escrow was to close in May. We also had a new puppy. She was a Lhasa Apso and our girls fell in love with her. She was given to us by June and Jim Perry who owned the mother. We called her Sacha and she soon became a member of our family.

In May, Jana had her big day as she was baptized in Chatsworth. Amada and Bob Sena, neighbors in Chatsworth, were the Godparents.

We began spending long weekends in San Clemente at our new house. We had lots of guests and before long we felt like permanent citizens of the beach community. I began to think of the possibility of living there full time.

We did take a little time off from vacationing at the beach to take a family vacation in mid-July in Buffalo. I did some research on Snake Oil Johnny while I was there. I was beginning to write the screenplay which one day would be the basis of a projected series based on his life.

In August, Eric Scott and I, with the strong backing of Don Ralke, did our show at the Multnomah County Fair in Portland. The governor was in attendance and Bill Cosby had the same stage the night before us. We were in fast company.

The seventh season of *The Waltons* rolled right along with almost every

Louise and I with our daughters Jana (left) and Erin (right), and our family dog Sacha (a Lhasa Apso).

story having Ronnie Claire and I having strong input. It became almost automatic to read the script and being impressed with the amount of time *The Waltons* were giving to the Godseys.

In fall I was able to rent our San Clemente house for the winter. We would return in June of 1980. The rent was break-even.

CHAPTER NINETEEN

The Ninth Season?

The ninth season was scheduled to start shooting in June. As usual and normally the cast would be notified around May 1 that our options were being activated. However, the rumor mil was hyperactive. Our numbers, per the Neilson ratings, were not exciting. Not being at the studio every day, the news was verbal, mostly over the phone lines. I was in contact with Eric and he had heard that the show wasn't going to be continued. To quote our sister show, *Eight Is Enough*, everything must end sooner or later and it looked as if *The Waltons* had reached its limit. It was a fact that Richard Thomas was gone. He might appear in a show or two as he had done in the past, but as a series regular, he had no interest. Michael Learned was active in the second season of her own series, *Nurse*. Will Geer had passed away. And Ellen Corby had been silenced by her stroke. The only one left of the five stars of 1972 was Ralph Waite. I'm sure the executives of CBS were contemplating pulling the plug on our show because the stars of the show had abdicated for one reason or the other. In late May I was notified that my option was being picked up and the ninth season was about to be underway. I was ecstatic.

But the Screen Actors Guild threatened strike and then it materialized. The family plan was to spend the entire summer in San Clemente and I was to take the train back and forth. I was to have a car parked near the train station in downtown L.A and to drive that back and forth from Chatsworth to the studio. But then SAG called the strike and my transportation situation never occurred. We were in our vacation home almost exclusively with the show on hold. The strike was wonderful for us personally allowing us to spend most of the summer at the beach. But I knew that it was a great hardship for many. I hoped for a quick settlement, but it took months.

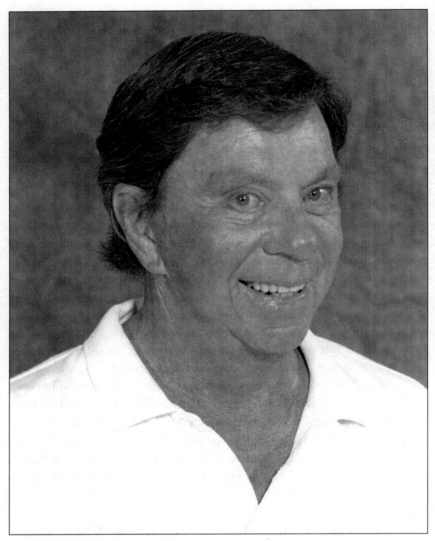

A publicity photo, from about 1980.

During that summer of 1980, I received an offer from the VFW to receive an award at their yearly convention which was being held in Chicago. The offer was to fly Louise and I to Chicago first class and to put us up at the Conrad Hilton for a couple of nights. I was to receive their Spirit of America Award and to speak to their general assembly. The date for this trip was August 20, 1980. Louise didn't wish to go but suggested that I take Erin as my guest. Louise felt that it would give me a chance to bond with her. In addition, Louise would be able to spend a few days exclusively with Jana. It sounded good to me.

Erin was wonderful to travel with. She was wide-eyed; everything was new and exciting to her. Arriving at O'Hare, we were picked up in a limo and delivered to the hotel. We were welcomed by an officer of the VFW and taken to our room which just happened to be the presidential suite. It had been occupied by Ronald and Nancy Reagan the previous night when the VFW had endorsed him for president. The suite was about 1,800 square feet. (Yes, I paced it off.) It had two bedrooms, three baths, a dining room, a kitchen and a living room. It also had three giant-size TVs. I was told that I wouldn't be needed until noon the next day and our time was our own until then. We had dinner in the dining room and then decided to take a walk as it was still light at about 8:00 P.M. We walked outside and Erin looked all about then asked her question which I have never been able to forget.

"Where's the sky, Daddy?"

Eight-year-old Erin and I were surrounded by skyscrapers. I pointed directly up and, sure enough, there it was way up there. She smiled. The Loop in Chicago is perhaps even more dramatic than New York City. The hundreds of big hotels and office buildings occupy a smaller area. The sidewalks and nearby parks were loaded with convention merrymakers.

The following morning, after breakfast, we took in some sights, including the Sears Tower which, at 110 stories, was the tallest building in the world. Up in the observation tower it was possible to see the state of Michigan, which was fifty miles across the lake. At least I thought we could see it.

Back in the hotel, Erin and I dressed for our appearance. I tried to brush her hair like Mommy would do but I don't think I was as successful. But she looked cute anyway. The phone rang and someone from the VFW notified me that they would welcome me at the mezzanine level. Erin and I were met by officials and an honor guard marched us into the auditorium then right up on the stage. The VFW Ladies Auxiliary president introduced Erin and then me. She then presented the award and read the inscription: "To Joe Conley for his volunteer leadership and service in the American Cancer Society saving lives, strengthening America. Star of TV and films, he has brought millions of hours of happiness to millions of people. As Ike on *The Waltons*, he has fostered high moral principles bolstering the American way of life. When his country called, he answered, served with bravery as an US Army Artillery Lt., decorated with the Purple Heart and Silver Star. He lives his patriotism every day."

The audience gave me a standing ovation. I looked over at Erin as she smiled from ear to ear. Her daddy was being honored. I hadn't anticipated such an award and I was actually speechless for a minute. However, I did recover my composure and spoke to the audience with honest humility. It was the most salutary honor I had ever received other than the Silver Star and I didn't exactly try to win that one.

That afternoon and early evening Erin and I did a little more sightseeing then returned home the next morning.

A few weeks later, the SAG strike was settled and we returned to work. I never did get the experience of taking the train from San Clemente to downtown L.A. Erin and Jana returned to school and our summer at San Clemente was over. We sold the house a couple of months later.

The ninth season was a dream come true for me. Each week the Godseys looked forward to a new script in which we were featured. Our billing had been improved to "also starring" and some weeks Ronnie Claire and I had our own starring vehicle. The show could have been *The Godseys* rather than *The Waltons*.

One particular memory still makes me laugh, even today. One morning, a group of cast and crew members were sitting in a big circle just gabbing as we waited for the set to be dressed and lighted. Somehow the topic of the conversation turned to dreams. I told of my dream the previous night when I had been notified that I was being drafted to serve in the Vietnam War. I related that I protested vehemently that I had served in two wars already. But the draft board persisted and my nightmare continued until the alarm clock awakened me.

Everybody laughed at my dream except Dick Chaffee, our script supervisor. He asked me if I had read the following week's script. I told him no, I hadn't received it yet. He chuckled to himself and predicted that I would enjoy the read.

A few days later I received the next script and, lo and behold, Ike Godsey was being called into WWII. Ike received his notice and promptly threw it away; it was obviously a mistake. Shortly after that, an FBI agent appeared at the store and arrested Ike for draft-dodging and took him away. Ike was taking his physical when John Walton appeared on the scene and testified that I was born in 1900, not 1920. It was a funny script and I'll never forget my dream which was a coincidence that I would never believe if I hadn't been there.

Another script, entitled "The Pearls," featured Corabeth and her twin. Ronnie Claire played both roles and caused great consternation for Ike. A script entitled "The Indiscretion" had Ike suffering through the discovery by Corabeth that Ike had had an affair. Finally the truth came out that the events took place before their marriage.

The following season was a surprise for all of us when CBS failed to pick up the option for another season. The producers went to the rival network, NBC, and got them to authorize a short season of three two-hour shows written around a wedding, Mother's Day and Thanksgiving. These shows were to be shot over a six-week period in late 1981. In the early fall of 1981, I was in New York pitching to literary agents a novel I had written. Richard Thomas was appearing on Broadway. When I talked to him backstage, I supplied him with the news I had just received of the NBC shows. He told me that he wouldn't be in the cast. Whether he had been asked to play in them or not I did not know.

The shooting went very well. Then in January of 1982 my agent called me and had an offer for me to star in *Last of the Red Hot Lovers*, a super play written by Neil Simon, in a dinner theater in Winnipeg, Canada. Rehearsals were to start on March 4 and the run was to be eight weeks closing in late May. I accepted the offer after Louise and I discussed it and arranged for her to visit for a week in early April, during Easter week, when the girls were on Easter holiday.

The role was challenging one as I was on stage every minute. The protagonist (my role) is in middle age and realizes that he has never had an affair. So, in the three acts, he attempts, in his silly way, to have a sexual involvement with three different women. The show went well, receiving good reviews, and the family visit was a wonderful experience.

When I arrived in Winnipeg, it was near the end of a typical frigid winter. When I left in late May, it was approaching summer time. The last few weeks I was able to play a lot of golf and enjoy my stay. I met many wonderful people.

During the run of *The Waltons* I hired several publicity agents. Their purpose was to provide me with good press and to keep my name before the public. The best PR person I had was Cynthia Snyder. We are sill friends today. One day she called me and suggested that I give an interview to a reporter from *The National Inquirer*. I was surprised that she would suggest an interview with a paper that was considered a sleazy rag, primarily involved with sex, divorce and immoral and dishonest activity by persons of some notoriety. Cynthia explained to me that the reporter who she worked with was a person of high moral character who wouldn't waste his time with skuzzy lies. "If he did, he would lose all credibility with PR people," explained Cynthia. "He'll tape the interview and give you a copy. He will use only the material on the tape for his story." I agreed to the interview.

About a week later, I met with the reporter poolside at our home. Although I was still just a little bit unsure, the reporter was dressed well, soft spoken and asked good questions. He provided me with a tape of the interview as promised.

A few weeks later I pulled up in front of the boy's dormitory where my son, Kevin, was enrolled. He and several classmates were standing there waiting to be picked up. Kevin and I were going out to dinner. On entering the car, his first statement to me was, "We were just reading about you in the *Inquirer*." I asked what was the article was about. The reporter had covered several topics.

Kevin had a sort of smirk on his face as he answered. "The topic was about you being drunk and falling off a float in a parade."

I nearly swallowed my gum in reaction. "What?"

Kevin quoted the article as best he could. However, he didn't have a copy of the newspaper. I drove to the nearest supermarket and bought a copy. Over dinner I read the article in its entirety. It was a scandalous article that said in three different ways that I was drunk and fell off a float at the San Gabriel Christmas Parade. The only truth in the article was the fact that I had been on a float in that parade. I tried my best to explain to Kevin what had transpired. Ronnie Claire Edwards and I were on a float together. At one point in the parade the float came to a complete stop. I saw a man selling popcorn to the crowd. I jumped off the float then ran over to the popcorn guy and bought a bag. I was hungry and hadn't eaten since lunch seven or eight hours earlier. Getting back on the float, I had one leg up on the float and the other one on the street as the float started up. I fell back and almost went under the wheel but I managed to dodge the tire as the float rode merrily on. The driver was unaware of my fall. I laughed in relief as Ronnie and I snacked on popcorn and waved happily to the crowd. My alcoholic intake that night had been about three ounces of white wine which was provided for us in a car dealer's showroom as we awaited the parade startup. I was cold sober and did not fall off a float. The article was totally false. Kevin did not comment. I don't know whether he believed me or not. I experienced up close and personal the evils of malicious publicity. I wondered how my producers would react. Could it affect my career? I spoke with Louise about the article when I got back from Ojai. She was concerned but not as bent out of shape as I was. She didn't seem to think it would have any effect on me.

Louise said, "The people who read that kind of drivel don't have any control over your job!" Her opinion helped soothe me but, to make sure, I would get on the subject first thing in the morning.

However, before I could make any calls the next day I received two.

The first call was from Ronnie Claire. She was very upset about the article and volunteered to set anyone straight. "You weren't drunk and you didn't fall off the float. I'd demand a retraction."

The second call was from my PR person, Cynthia Snyder. She had been in contact with the writer who did the interview with me. He denied any knowledge of the story about the parade. He explained to Cynthia that the Inquirer used "stringers," freelance writers, who sold articles to various publications. That was probably the source. I told Cynthia to demand a retraction.

Several days later she got back to me with word from *The Inquirer*. They had discovered that the stringer made up his story. The editor apologized, but it was against their policy to retract. However, they promised to write several positive articles about me.

Regarding the demand for retraction, I spoke to an attorney. He explained that to sue for scandal and malicious gossip would be very difficult to win. I would have to prove financial loss. Regarding their promise to write several positive stories about me, they kept their word. They published two articles about me. Both of them used information from the interview. To the best of my knowledge, the article never harmed me. But it sure caused me some sleepless nights at the time.

When the series ended in January of 1982, I hoped to move on to another series or features. This didn't occur. Yes, I did a few TV shows and a feature or two but not the level of activity that I wished for. I did a bunch of TV and radio commercials over a three-year period for a market chain in Northern California. In 1993 and 1997 *The Waltons* did two 2-hour Movies of the Week for CBS. Richard Thomas returned to the fold and starred in both of them. I was told by Earl Hamner that a third show featuring Ike when his store burned down had been written and approved by CBS. But time passed and executives changed and it was never made.

Ike Godsey was created by Earl Hamner, and lived on the screen from 1971 until 1997 — twenty-six years. The character still lives in reruns on a number of cable channels.

In 1996, I was paired with what's-his-name. His initials are "TW."

However, Joe Conley lives on through the present until some unknown date in the future. People ask me if I am retired and I smilingly answer them, "Actors don't retire, they die. And I haven't died yet." This retort usually gets a laugh. But if I were to be honest with myself I have to admit that I am retired. I no longer have an agent; I no longer go on interviews, and no longer read *Variety* or *The Hollywood Reporter*. My career is probably over. However, I would work again if given the opportunity. My career had one major highlight and that was playing Ike Godsey on *The Waltons*.

Louise and I live on a hill overlooking the 8th green of a golf course and the two of us play two or three times a week. My game is not very good but I still enjoy playing. Louise enjoys beating me, which she does most of the time. Both of our kids are doing fine in life. We see them both very often. And we have two grandchildren: Maddy Lou and Max Joseph. They are the children of Erin and Tom Pieronek and are the light of Louise's eyes. I think they are pretty special, too. We travel a lot, but are always happy to get back home. I enjoy going to the activities that our fan club arranges. Eric Scott and I are still good friends. We meet for lunch about once a month. I used to tell people that I planned to die on the set. That still sounds like a pretty good way to go but I was just joking around. It's been a very good life. My health is excellent. I don't plan on leaving but when the good Lord calls, I'll accept the call. But Ike Godsey will live on as long as they have DVDs or tape players. Ike was a pretty good guy even if I say so myself, and Walton's Mountain was a good place to spend those many years. And I thank my wife, Louise, for making our marriage the finest I could ever imagine.

That reminds me of an old joke in which a famous comedian, George Burns, was asked why he was so certain that that he'd live to be 100. George answered, "I have to; I'm booked."

The Conley clan on holiday in Hawaii in June of 2009. Joe is at nine o'clock. Following clockwise are daughter Jana, Louise, daughter Erin Pieronek, granddaughter Maddy and son in law, Tom Pieronek. Grandson Max asks, "What's going on?"

Lightning Source UK Ltd.
Milton Keynes UK
UKOW03f2150180713

214044UK00014B/486/P